ISBN 978-1-334-00813-9
PIBN 10749752

This book is a reproduction of an important historical work. Forgotten Books uses state-of-the-art technology to digitally reconstruct the work, preserving the original format whilst repairing imperfections present in the aged copy. In rare cases, an imperfection in the original, such as a blemish or missing page, may be replicated in our edition. We do, however, repair the vast majority of imperfections successfully; any imperfections that remain are intentionally left to preserve the state of such historical works.

For support please visit www.forgottenbooks.com

1 MONTH OF
FREE
READING

at

www.ForgottenBooks.com

By purchasing this book you are eligible for one month membership to ForgottenBooks.com, giving you unlimited access to our entire collection of over 700,000 titles via our web site and mobile apps.

To claim your free month visit:

www.forgottenbooks.com/free749752

English
Français
Deutsche
Italiano
Español
Português

www.forgottenbooks.com

Mythology Photography **Fiction**
Fishing Christianity **Art** Cooking
Essays Buddhism Freemasonry
Medicine **Biology** Music **Ancient
Egypt** Evolution Carpentry Physics
Dance Geology **Mathematics** Fitness
Shakespeare **Folklore** Yoga Marketing
Confidence Immortality Biographies
Poetry **Psychology** Witchcraft
Electronics Chemistry History **Law**
Accounting **Philosophy** Anthropology
Alchemy Drama Quantum Mechanics
Atheism Sexual Health **Ancient History**
Entrepreneurship Languages Sport
Paleontology Needlework Islam
Metaphysics Investment Archaeology
Parenting Statistics Criminology
Motivational

REFUTATION

OF THE

ARGUMENT A PRIORI

FOR THE

BEING AND ATTRIBUTES OF GOD;

SHOWING

THE IRRELEVANCY OF THAT ARGUMENT,

AS WELL AS THE

FALLACIOUS REASONING

OF

DR. SAMUEL CLARKE AND OTHERS,

ESPECIALLY OF

MR GILLESPIE,

IN SUPPORT OF IT.

BY

ANTITHEOS.

" AUDI ALTERAM PARTEM."

" A man that is first in his own cause seemeth right, but his neighbour cometh after him and searcheth him."

" In the present instance, as in all others, there is not a single position taken in hostility to antitheistical principles, that will not also be found hostile, either to physical science or sound philosophy."

GLASGOW:

PRINTED AND PUBLISHED BY H. ROBINSON & CO.,

7, BRUNSWICK PLACE,

For the Glasgow Zetetic Society,

AND SOLD BY THE BOOKSELLERS.

1838.

LC Control Number

tmp96   029153

PREFACE.

THE circumstance which has unexpectedly called forth the following refutation is somewhat remarkable. A gentleman who, in 1833, published a volume, entitled, "An Argument a priori for the Being and Attributes of God," sent a *challenge*, a few months ago, to a society of freethinkers in this city, " to refute the reasoning contained in the aforesaid work." The tone of the communication is rather fierce than gallant; haughty and cavalier rather than courteous. Perhaps the author, in his zeal of God, does not conceive any great civility to be due to those who do not subscribe to his own creed. If so, it is only another instance among the many that occur, of men, even men of learning and talents, allowing a morose religion to hold the sway over their better nature.

Mr Gillespie, the author of the argument alluded to, had been disappointed, it seems, in finding an antagonist elsewhere, notwithstanding his anxious endeavours to provoke opposition. The gauntlet was thrown down, but no one was fully prepared to take it up. This may have been the ground of his confidence, and of his almost triumphant anticipations of submission in all against whom he might think proper to assume a hostile bearing. If, however, hearty and fair opposition be all that he desires, *that* object of his wishes is now offered him as some compensation for his former disappointments.

It may nevertheless of all this be mentioned, that the challenge was accepted—not exactly to gratify Mr Gillespie —nor because any of the individuals appealed to in the affair, held himself bound to lift the gage, or answer any call to refute opinions contrary to his own,—but because one of them had long since purposed to write some time or other upon the subject. This was at least the principal motive. Another might be to vindicate openly avowed freethinkers from the charge (implied in the gentleman's letter) of incompetency to such a task. The letter itself indeed might here have been inserted verbatim,—only that a considerable proportion of it consists of irrelevant matter, besides containing passages which could by no means militate in favor of the writer, but of which his respondent wishes to take no advantage.

This article might have been restricted to the consideration of Mr. Gillespie's work, and to that alone. Indeed, in the note addressed to Mr. G. intimating that his argument would be replied to, nothing was stated of any other course being contemplated. But on second thoughts, it was conceived that this would be to narrow the thing too much. Other writers have signalized themselves in the treatment of the greatest question in theology by the argument a priori : —and it might have been said with justice, and without disparagement to any one,—that such a reply would have been very defective, as overlooking the first and greatest authority in the case. A supplementary answer, it is true, might have been made to follow; but this plan of publication is both awkward and inconvenient, and moreover, it would not have squared so well with the original intention already expressed.

It has further to be noticed, that in replying to the argument a priori, it would be unreasonable to expect every thing to be brought under consideration which the authors who have adopted this strain of reasoning, have chosen to introduce. In strict conformity with logical principle, perhaps, they ought not to be followed one step " out of the record," however far they may wander from it. I shall as seldom as possible deviate from this principle; yet, if on an occasion, a plausible argument be found thrust in, having no proper place in what is going forward, I trust I shall be excused for attending to it, on the ground that it is safer to do too much in this way than too little,—especially as it is too commonly apt to be supposed, that an argument unanswered is one that is unanswerable.

GLASGOW, 15th Dec. 1837.

CONTENTS.

CHAPTER I.

Character and Irrelevancy of the Argument.

To hear of the existence of a god being made the subject of demonstration by argument, is altogether astounding. The announcement, on the other hand, sounds so oddly, as to mitigate the effect of the first impression, if not to excite ridicule at the wonderful discrepancy between the end in view, and the means laid out for the attainment of it. Habit, however, reconciles people to the greatest absurdities; and the approval of the argument *a priori* by a considerable proportion—it might be added, the most erudite and enlightened—of the Christian world, compels us to regard it with more deference than its intrinsic merits deserve.

The legitimate mode of effecting any demonstration relative to the real existence of things, is by an exhibition of the thing itself whose existence is the subject of proof. Now, a god, in as far as this point is concerned, must be held as a real being; that is, his votaries, as a matter of course, maintain this to be the fact. This granted, argument appears quite out of place. It would never do to talk of proving the existence of the man in the moon by argument; neither would it be of any avail to employ a syllogism or a sorites to demonstrate the existence of a navigable channel between the Atlantic and Pacific oceans, through the arctic regions of America: yet if the reasoning under review be relevant, these must be so too. If an a priori argument be capable of proving the existence of one thing, another may be proved by the same, or any other logical process.

It may be accounted indecorous, perhaps, to refer such similes to the being of a god. But the tenderness of parties upon certain points whereabout they are apt to feel sore, is not to be taken as a reason why they should not be touched, even in attempting a cure. It is convenient, I dare say, to affect being pained, and to express dislike with respect to the idea of—reducing, I was going to say, but it really is—bringing up, the evidence to be admitted in proving the existence of a deity, to the level of that which is alone admissible in other cases of the same kind. It is even highly serviceable to the interests of religion, for its more acute and sensitive adherents to appear shocked themselves, and excite similar feelings in others, and the passions consequent upon them, at any such proposal as that now hinted at. Why people should be shocked, however, why they should either be disgusted or pained, I cannot well perceive, unless it be merely from prejudice; for the nature of the subject of probation certainly requires some small support from the evidence of the senses.

This kind of demonstration, all the theology of all the religions in the world, cannot afford. But if a god is never to be seen now-a-days, as is pretended to have been the case in former times, we are told to look to Nature, where we may see God in his works. This is the common and more fashionable way of discussing the great question before us, which has prevailed from Philo's time to the present. It is called the argument *a posteriori*: it relies on experience, and deduces causes from their effects. This process, however, is quite illogical, and, although it were otherwise, is of no great utility in its operation. It takes for granted the existence of an agent capable of producing the effects contemplated as the source of the argument—which of course is begging the principle — and only attempts to make out power, and wisdom, and goodness, and so forth, to be proper attributes of that agent. As Mr Gillespie himself has well observed, it cannot prove wisdom, goodness, power, or any other divine attribute to be unlimited. Assuming the existence of a god, it cannot demonstrate that he has always existed; it cannot demonstrate that he must exist eternally, nor even prove that that existence may not have already terminated. A clock continues to indicate the lapse of time, although the hand that set it in motion has ceased to be animate.

The idea of so grievous a defect inherently attaching to evidence so much relied upon, was not to be endured, and some of the consequences, although barely glanced at, were too horrid for contemplation. Up starts the logician of the new school, therefore, with a remedy for this great evil. A scheme is devised of making every point at issue a matter of rigid demonstration. The most exalted view of the divine character is to be taken. All the attributes of deity are to be drawn to the largest scale—nay, magnified to infinitude itself, and borne out in a manner the most absolute, as well as his eternity both past and future. It is irrefragably to be proved, not only that a god *does* exist, but that he *must* exist, and that too as necessarily as that two and two make four ;—that his non-existence, in short, cannot even be conceived !

A vast project this is, most undoubtedly; demanding powers and ingenuity equally vast to execute. Like the dogma of all things being created out of nothing, to which, indeed, this argument is strongly allied, the thing seems impossible. Maugre every impediment, however, the attempt is boldly made. A being existing by necessity is sought for ; that is (according to the new logic) one whose non-existence it is not in the power of man to imagine; simple in its essence ; indivisible: everywhere present, and without which nothing else can be supposed to exist. To seek in nature for such a being ; to ransack the whole universe for it were vain. Among real and known existences it was nowhere to be found. But the brain of the theologue, like the lanthorn of Diogenes, was set to discover what the sun could not reveal; and if equally honest with the cynic, his imitator would have been every whit as unsuccessful. Those who contrive an object for search, however, know precisely where to find it. Hence, the reasoner of the anti-experimental sect having laid up the thing cut and dry, in his own conceptions, brought it forth with an air of triumph due to a great discovery.

It could not escape observation among minds of an abstract and reflective turn, that space possesses some of the attributes commonly ascribed to deity, such as infinity, and, of course, omnipresence; immateriality, and so forth: that duration cannot be supposed to have had a beginning, or to be within the possibility of ever coming to an end. It must thus have appeared to the metaphysical theist, exceedingly desirable to bring these idle and unappropriated attributes into more useful play, and in a manner the most advantageous to the common faith. Clarke and Butler, and all their followers, have accordingly talked much of these matters, and evinced a strong predilection for them in selecting examples wherewithal to illustrate the absolute and infinite perfections of the divine nature. These metaphysicians, in short, have made space and duration usurp the station and dignity of a divine being. They have taken this empty and inanimate fabrication, and set it up in a newly-erected shrine of curiously mathematical construction, and fallen down to it as the god of their idolatry.

If the theory be vague and visionary which the argument a priori is introduced to support, it is not to be expected that the argument itself should be of a different character. A false principle cannot well be maintained by reasoning which is true. The truth is, the argument in question is nothing else than an attempt to establish the application of mathematical reasoning to what it has nothing in earth or heaven to do with,—namely, real existences; at least what is held to be real by those who employ such argument. But how vain and preposterous the attempt! As well might it be maintained, that as the whole is in the abstract a perfect quantity, it must contain within itself all the qualities of the different parts of which it is composed; that as some of these parts are small and some large, some round and some square, some black and some white; it must be white and black, and square and round, and large and small at the same time! Aristotelians inform us, that every sound argument is capable of being reduced to the syllogistic form. If so, I should be glad to hear from their own lips an exemplification in the present case. To my own untrained thinking, it should run somewhat thus:—

Whatever necessarily possesses absolute perfections is God;

Metaphysical abstractions possess absolute perfections;—
Therefore, metaphysical abstractions are God.

If this be not a fair statement of the whole argument in the most logical form, I am at a loss to know what is. Should it be any way wrong, and should some ardent disciple of the metaphysical school of theology deign hereafter to take a part in this discussion, it would be well were he to consult the Stagyrite and correct it. In any event, our reasoners a priori have either to acknowledge the absurdity here set forth in mood and figure, or deny that they appropriate abstract reasoning to questions of ontological science. If their god be a real being—an agent, he cannot be a heap of abstractions: if made up of abstractions, he cannot be an agent. No reasoning imaginable can make him both : yet to nothing short of working out this impossibility does the argument aim.

It must be granted, indeed, that such parts of the process as have a bearing upon the divine actions, as well as those which go to establish the moral and intellectual character of deity, do not properly belong to the argument a priori. These things are either boldly thrust in where they are out of all keeping, or humbly introduced in forma pauperis, and so made to pass off with the rest. But after all, and with every advantage, fair and foul, that can be claimed for it, it is at best but a sorry piece of patch work. Restricted to its own province, it can prove nothing, demonstrate nothing to be either true or false but what is *necessarily* so, in the most abstract and mathematical sense of the terms.

Here, indeed, the grand secret in managing the argument before us lies. It affixes a partial and out-of-the-way meaning to words, especially those upon which the whole question turns, and so, misconstrues and misapplies general language. *Necessity*, for instance, which by the way is the keystone of the structure, is different from what it is found to be anywhere else, except, perhaps, in some other region of mere speculation. In the premises, it is attenuated to the utmost fineness of its mathematical acceptation, although the weight of its common and real meaning is essential to the validity of the conclusion. *Substance,* in like manner, is totally dissimilar to any thing known by that name. It seems an evanescent, or rather imperceptible—nothing; yet, lo !' it is found in the end that something substantial was after all to be understood.

These things, however, will be more clearly apprehended when we come to discuss the logic of this strange argument in detail. In the meantime it may not be amiss to show, that the character of irrelevancy here laid at the door of the a priori argument, is not unwarranted by the authority of good judges among the religious themselves. Abundance of quotations might be adduced, but I shall content myself with an extract from the Edinburgh Review for October 1830, (vol. lii. p. 113,) in an article upon Dr Morehead's "Dialouges on Natural and Revealed Religion." That the reviewer reasons upon theistical principles is evident from the allusion he makes to "the will of the creator," to which, I may remark in passing, he allows the most orthodox latitude. Relative to our argument a priori he observes :— " The truth is, it involves a radical fallacy which not only renders it useless but dangerous to the cause it is intended to support. The question as to the being of a god, is purely a question of fact : he either exists or he does not exist. But there is an evident absurdity in pretending to demonstrate a matter of fact, or to prove it by argument a priori ; because nothing is demonstrable unless the contrary implies a contradiction, and this can never be predicated. of the negative of any proposition which merely affirms or asserts a matter of fact. Whatever we conceive as existent, we can also conceive as non-existent, and consequently there is no being whose non-existence implies a contradiction, or, in other words, whose existence is a priori demonstrable. This must be evident to every one who knows what demonstration really means. It is a universal law, that all heavy bodies descend to the earth in a line directed towards its centre; But the contrary of this may easily be conceived, because it involves no contradiction ; for bodies might have fallen upward, if we may so express it, as well as downward,

had such been the will of the creator. But we cannot con_
ceive the opposite of one of the demonstrated truths of geo_
metry, as, for example, that the three angles of a triangle
should be either greater or less than two right angles, be_
cause this implies a contradiction. The distinction, there_
fore, between necessary or demonstrable truths and matters
of fact, consists in this,—that the contrary of the former
involves a contradiction, whereas that of the latter does not.
But there is no contradiction implied in conceiving the non-
existence of the deity; and therefore his existence is not a
necessary truth, a priori demonstrable."

To add any thing to the foregoing reasoning of the
reviewer were perhaps superfluous. It is clear and satisfactory. Yet I cannot well refrain from taking notice of a
single circumstance by way of illustration. Men have often
been made to suffer severely—on some occasions to the loss
of life—for denying the being of a god, while the great mass
of the people, so far from regarding these occurrences as
either absurd or unjust, have looked on them as well-merited
punishments. But was ever any one put to death, or sent
to the pillory, for denying that twice two make four? The
idea, indeed, is ridiculous; but wherefore should it be so ?
Simply because *it is not possible* there should be any difference of opinion about the matter. If, however, the dogmas
of theology, or even say the primary one, were capable of
demonstration as mathematical doctrines are, there could be
no difference in the respect due to doubts and denials in
either case; or rather, it would be impossible to find doubt-
ers and deniers in the one more than in the other. I do not
mention the horrid penalties awarded in our barbarous laws
to certain kinds of unbelief, in proof of the real importance
of the articles of faith they have been enacted to maintain
by brute force. Statutes of this description are a proof of
nothing but legislative ignorance and the persecuting nature
of the religions they have been made to defend. Their very
existence, however, as well as that of the stupid prejudices,
alas ! but too prevalent, upon which they are founded, are
totally incompatible with the validity of that mode of argu-

ment which would demonstrate the being of a god upon abstract principles.

But the propositions and reasonings of the different authors who have adopted the mode of procedure now shown to be directed so wide of the mark, must not be passed over without special notice. It is more easy to censure an argument in general terms, than to meet all its particular parts on fair and open grounds. Even this labour, therefore, I cheerfully undertake, that there may be nothing left to suppose on the score of disingenuousness or pretended want of interest in the matter. No one can be more fully aware than I am, of how nearly this discussion approaches in some points to a verbal dispute. But what of that? If the religious world choose to peril their cause on grounds so insecure, upon themselves let the dishonour of perverting things from their right purposes, and all its consequences, fall. Be it always remembered, too, that this argument of theirs, has repeatedly been put forth as unanswerable, and that according to their own showing, the mighty problem of the being of a god depends upon the result.

———

CHAP. II.

Fallacies of Dr Clarke's Demonstration.

In examining the reasonings of the theologians who have advocated the fundamental articles of their creed upon a priori principles, the " Demonstration of the being and attributes of God," by Dr Samuel Clarke, demands our first attention. This much is due to the reverend divine on account of his acknowledged talents and great reputation, as well as the early appearance of his work. His Demonstration has been too long before the public, and ranks too high as a standard theological production, to require particular description here. This celebrated treatise is stated in twelve propositions, supported severally by such arguments as the author must have deemed best calculated for that purpose.

He introduces his subject by assigning certain causes for the existence of atheism. These he specifies to be excessive ignorance and stupidity; or vicious habits; or, at best, false philosophy.

It is perhaps hardly worth while to contend about these matters; yet it may be observed, that if some savage tribes, as inferior in intelligence as they are represented, have no notion or belief of the being of a god; a greater number, to the full as ignorant and stupid, possess abundance of credulity upon the subject; and if we go to what is called civilised life, the most ignorant and debased are not only religious, but generally the most firmly fixed in their faith. The second class of persons mentioned,—men who from their evil practices have been led to scoff at every thing religious—are not atheists at all. Such characters always show, in the hour of suffering and in the prospect of death, that they had never been thoroughly convinced of the falsehood of religion, but only that it marred their merriment and discountenanced their wickedness. The form and profession of faith thrown aside recklessly and without consideration, the essence remains. It lies dormant for a time, till the storm of passion which crushed it to a certain extent has subsided, when it springs into activity more powerfully than ever. Slavishness to the appetites can never convince the understanding. It may drive men to *disregard* religion, as well as every thing else of a serious nature, but it cannot make them *disbelievers*. Disregarders and disbelievers, however, are very different characters.

As to the philosophy which leads to atheism being false, *that* is the very question to be tried in the sequel. Of those, however, who take philosophy as the basis of their unbelief, the Doctor has a preliminary concession to demand; namely, that the being of a god is very desirable. The demand is made that they should " be very willing, nay, desirous above all things to be convinced that their present opinion is an error." But what opinion must be formed of the goodness of a cause or the soundness of an argument, when it is found necessary either to beg or demand a predisposition in its favor ? The frame of mind most proper and most adequate to judge of any matter, is to be without desire or predisposition of any kind, whether for or against it. Any other, indeed, is prejudicial. Let us hear, however, what his reverence has to urge for the necessity of this concession.

" Man of himself," says he, " is infinitely insufficient for his own happiness ; he is liable to many evils and miseries, which he can neither prevent nor redress ; he is full of wants which he cannot supply, and compassed about with infirmities which he cannot remove, and obnoxious to dangers which he can never sufficiently provide against, &c. Under which evil circumstances it is evident there can be no sufficient support but in the belief of a wise and good God."

To make this case worth a rush, it ought to have been shewn that the faithful are exempted, and none else, from the calamities here complained of. If the belief of a god, or even the real existence of such a being, is not to relieve me of my infirmities and wretchedness, why should either the one or the other be any way desirable to me ? What earthly good can it do a man environed with woes and worn down with misery, to be assured that a god exists who either cannot or will not afford him relief ? Has it not rather a strong tendency to excite his chagrin ? A god so poor and useless as to be unable to afford him relief, could only be an object of reproach and contempt ; and one who could, but would not, must appear too odious and malevolent in character to be regarded with other feelings than fear—if not hatred and aversion. The incredulous man is, on the contrary, much more comfortably situated. If he suffers,—he estimates the causes, whether moral or physical, according to their own character, without looking into the terra incognito for some supposed agency to account for them. He is not like the child who beats the floor for hurting him when he falls, or kisses for not breaking his bones.

If ever Dr Clarke studied the interesting subject of the origin of evil, or even thought or read upon it, he seems to have forgotten all ; for the above argument is given with the most admirable simplicity, although it evidently militates di-

rectly against himself. It is as much as to say, There is a
dreadful deal of evil in the world, and we cannot get quit of
it by any efforts of our own; but these very circumstances
render it imperative on the athiest to wish that the doctrine
he is opposed to were true, since in that case he would have
a god disinclined to remedy the evil, or as incapable of doing
it as himself.—What ! says the unbeliever, convince us by
our sufferings that we should like to have a god upon whom
to father them ! This is certainly a new-fashioned way of
paying compliment to deity. The author, to be sure, afterwards talks about the happiness of a hereafter, but to allude
to a matter as admitted, which does not even follow as a
consequence upon what he has yet to prove, is preposterous
in the extreme; more especially when, with regard to the
primary point, he is only pleading for a favorable reception
of what he has to offer in evidence.—But we must now recur
to Dr Clarke's propositions.

His first, that " *something has existed from eternity,*" no
one can object to. It carries its evidence along with it, and
must indeed be as cordially agreed to by the antitheist as the
most devout christian. The second, however, does not stand
in the same predicament. It is this, " *There must have existed from eternity some one unchangeable and independent
being.*"

I need say nothing of the alteration of the subject in the
present proposition from that of the preceding. It is perhaps
of little consequence any farther than indicating a certain
leaning; for which there ought to have been shewn some sort
of warrant. Was the mere *something* in the one case, not
sufficiently pregnant in meaning to sustain the weight of dignity awaiting the *being* in the other ? So at least it would
appear. What I particularly object to, however, is, that the
two terms in the predicate, " unchangeable and independent," are linked together as inseparable. The author does
not say one word in favor of this conjunction, and certainly
there is no necessity for it in the nature of things. In his
subsequent reasoning, he aims at establishing independence
alone; yet his conclusions are afterwards and all along drawn

as if both had been demonstrated. What are we to think of such a beginning? Precisely this,—that the reverend theorist was so intent upon making out his case in some sort, that an obstruction is overleaped with surprising facility, and a hiatus in his reasoning regarded as of no account.

With respect to the independence of the something which has always existed, the author's argument amounts to this: there must either be one being only of independent existence, or an infinite series of beings of dependent existence. But there cannot be an infinite series of the latter description. Therefore, there can only be one being of independent existence.—In support of his minor premiss, as here stated, Dr Clarke maintains that as no individual in the series can be the cause of itself, every one must have a cause, and if so, the whole must have a cause as well as the different parts. " If we consider," says he, " such an infinite progression as one entire endless series of dependent beings, it is plain this whole series of beings can have no cause from *without*, of its existence; because in it are supposed to be included all things that are or ever were in the universe: and it is plain it can have no reason *within* itself of its existence; because no one being in this infinite succession is supposed to be self-existent or necessary, but *every one* dependent on the foregoing; and where no *part* is necessary, it is manifest the *whole* cannot be necessary."

The fallacy here lies in the use of terms totally inept, and like the entire argument, inappropriate to the purpose. Is it not absurd to talk of anything being without or beyond infinity? and further, to make the whole force of a dilemma rest upon such absurdity? Is it not equally absurd to reason as if an endless series were to be regarded as made up of parts, *every one* of which may be taken into account? Did the metaphysician suppose, that by the introduction of his distributives and collectives, he had grasped the term of that which is infinite? He says (in effect), you have told me what the cause of the last individual of the series is, and of the one preceding that, and so on, but you have not told me what is the cause of the first. The reply—it is almost superfluous to say—is, that there can be no first, or any thing to leave an idea of priority in the mind.

Dr Clarke illustrates his argument by reference to an article extracted from Wollaston's Religion of Nature, comparing an infinite series to a chain " hung down out of heaven from an unknown height." But the chain in this instance is like all other things by which theists would bring us to concur in their imagined cause of an infinite series. The chain is evidently meant to be limited in extent. If not, what is to be understood by the allusion made by the writer to " what it hung upon?" The point of suspension, although at an unknown height, is certainly somewhere, and so, acts as a limitation to our views, and by consequence renders the simile useless. We may imagine the chain carried further off than where it is supposed to have hung from ; so that if it was infinite in its extent in the first case, it must be more than infinite in the second.

But what is the difference, after all, between an imaginary chain infinitely extended, and an imaginary rod extended in the same manner? If there be any difference relative to the point at issue, what is it? Yet the learned doctor would pronounce the one independent in its existence, and the other necessarily the reverse !

The author states the same case in another form ; but as this repetition of the argument is founded upon the fallacy which has just been exploded, of course it must share the fate of that which serves as its basis.

Dr Clarke himself seems half conscious of the inadequacy of his reasoning in demanding a cause for the existence of an infinite series, for he is reduced to the necessity of protesting, as it were, against the process by which he is baulked of his object. " It is only," he says, " a driving back from one step to another, and removing out of sight, the question concerning the ground or reason of the existence of things." What he adds about the series being neither self-existent nor necessary, is an unproved extravagance, the gist of which shall come under review in noticing the next proposition.— But here we may ask, if the same plea would not hold equally

good against a single being? If it had not existed yesterday, it could not exist to-day. Its continued existence, then,
depends upon its prior existence. If, however, it were ob-
jected, that to carry back the inquiry concerning the ground
or reason of its existence in this manner, would be to remove the question out of sight altogether,—what could the
doctor have answered that would not have " removed" his
own weak objection ?

Dr Clarke's third proposition is, that " *That unchangeable
and independent being which has existed from eternity without
any external cause of its existence, must be self-existent, that is,
necessarily existing.*"

At first sight this proposition appears to differ little from
the leading one. In glancing along what follows, however,
we perceive that more—much more, is meant than directly
meets the eye. Here, indeed, we have the epitome of the
whole argument. Here the author makes a wild, but determined assault upon the necessary existence of matter. Here
he brings out those subtle and incomprehensible theories relative to the divine nature of space and duration, and the
sine qua non of existence, which are so deeply interwoven
with the argument, and at the same time involved in dark-
ness and obscurity. And here too he summons up that
most potent—that eldest of all existences—NECESSITY, which
he subsequently exalts above all things; even " above all
that is called god and that is worshipped."—The truth is,
that the stress he has laid upon necessary existence is so
prodigious, that we are at a loss to see what he would be at.
Is it not enough that the eternal being should be proved
self-existent; that is, uncreated ? " No," says Dr Clarke in
the last words of his seventh reply to Butler;) " necessity is
the ground, or reason, or foundation of existence, both of
the divine substance and all the attributes ;" and in the pa-
ragraph preceding, he speaks of *that* necessity by which the
first cause exists ; and again, in his second letter, he declares
necessity to be " in itself original, absolute, and in the order
of nature, antecedent to all existence,"—so that, according to
this high authority, even the Great First Cause of all things,

(at least what the theist calls by this name,) could not exist —but for NECESSITY.

All this, of course, makes us somewhat curious to know what this mighty existence is, and it is so far fortunate that our curiosity does not go ungratified. We are told that it is anything the contrary of which it is a plain impossibility, or implying a contradiction to suppose: "for instance, the relation of equality between twice two and four is an absolute necessity, only because it is an immediate contradiction in terms to suppose them unequal. This," the author continues to observe, "is the only idea we can frame of absolute necessity; and to use the word in any other sense, seems to be using it without any signification at all."

Proceeding upon this partial, this extravagant view of the case, the reverend doctor sets about overthrowing the necessary existence of matter, by attempting to prove that there is such a thing in nature as a vacuum. The attempt, however, falls wretchedly short of its aim, depending as it does upon an lil-informed and very inadequate estimate of the properties of matter. On his knowledge of material things and their properties, it would almost be a want of charity to expose him. He makes no account of matter being of various descriptions, nor of the diversity of effects which must follow the operations of things so different as the different species of matter. "All bodies," he sagely observes, "being equally heavy, it follows necessarily that there must be a vacuum!"

The necessity of the sequence, I confess, I do not distinctly perceive; but suppose a vacuum granted,—what then?—that matter does not exist necessarily? Upon a priori principles, the theory of a vacuum was totally uncalled for. We can *conceive* matter not to exist, and that seems quite enough for the purpose. The purpose, however, goes too far: the argument, as already shown, proves too much. If matter is to be denied necessary existence because this supposition may be made respecting it, where is the single thing that can escape the same doom? Gods and devils, angels and spirits, heaven and hell,—supposing them all to exist—could have no claim to necessary existence, since it implies no contradiction to imagine them not to exist.

The self-existence which depends upon Dr Clarke's necessity, being thus a mere mathematical chimera, and no where to be found—no where in the world of realities—is a proof that there is something radically wrong in the argument. If such a condition as necessary or self-existence really exists, —why can it not be proved? Why can it not be made applicable to the material universe—to substance, the properties and operations of substance, and all that results from them? Because in these discussions a proper view of necessity never seems to have been taken. This is the reason, too, why Hume in his essay "Of the Idea of a Necessary Connexion," and after him, Dr Brown, in his "Observations" upon Mr Hume's doctrine concerning the relation of cause and effect, have fallen into such strange heresies in philosophy. In relation to physical subjects, they looked for mathematical necessity, and if they looked in vain, it is because their expectations were not founded in reason or the nature of things. This statement I shall now make good, and at the same time prove, which is more to the point, that matter is possessed of necessary existence.

That which is necessary, then, I would say, is obviously and simply, that which must be; that which is inevitable; that which is impossible not to be. It is useless to talk of that which is the contrary of an express contradiction. It is surely enough that upon every thing else than what is necessary, the stamp of impossibility is allowed to be set. Contraries and contradictions only belong to metaphysics and geometry. Mankind, however, were conversant with matters of common occurrence long before they became mathematicians or thought of soaring beyond physical things; and even yet, how few comparatively know any thing of abstract speculation or the use of its language. The usual acceptation of the word necessity, therefore, must be held the primary and essential acceptation; and that which would cut it down to the contrary of a contradiction, secondary and partial only. There is as absolute a necessity that a piece of wood should burn on being exposed to the action of fire, as there is for the equality between twice two and four. I shall be told that our ascertainment of the facts in these cases is derived from entirely different sources: that although experience be requisite in the one case, it is not so in the other; that besides, experience can never prove a thing necessary,—because while it is granted that each successive experiment increases the probabilities of a result similar to that which preceded, no number of probabilities can ever amount to a certainty.

To this I would reply, that the doctrine here laid down holds true in matters of chance, (for instance, the throwing of dice or the cutting of cards,) because the tendency and precision of the agency employed can never be perfectly ascertained, and therefore is to be left to the calculation of the different probabilities. It is quite otherwise, however, in the operations of nature. *There*, all is fixed and immutable as the truths of geometry themselves. An experiment once fairly and fully verified, nothing remains but to adopt the result as a determinate principle, from which there cannot possibly be the slightest deviation. Suppose a person to have been once or twice injured by burning, what should even the stickler for mathematical necessity think of this person, were he, nevertheless, to proceed upon the ground of there being no certainty,—but only a small chance, proportioned to the number of times he had suffered previously, —at any rate, no necessity of his again experiencing pain from the application of fire to his flesh? Both in the animal economy and in chemistry;—and indeed in every department of physical science,—in hydraulics, in electricity, in mechanics,—the nature and operation of a thing once being determined by adequate experience, uniform results are always accounted necessary. Sometimes, it is readily granted, our anticipations in these matters are not realized; that is, an experiment fails, but what of that? Would Dr Clarke himself have imputed the failure of an experiment to a want of stability in the laws of nature? No; but to the mismanagement of the operator, or else, to a difference in the causes that produced a difference in the effect. This uniform relation between cause and effect is what may fairly and properly be called physical necessity; and unless the laws of nature be variable and uncertain, that necessity is as absolute as it is that two and two should be four.

What now becomes of Dr Clarke's absolute necessity, which includes nothing but the reverse of what cannot be conceived?—which rejects as destitute of all meaning, whatever is not the opposite of a mathematical contradiction? We can conceive of a man (or three men as the scripture hath it) walking unharmed in the midst of a burning, fiery furnace. We can conceive of a man walking upon the fluctuating surface of the ocean, or mounting into the air—even taking a voyage to the moon and dog-star. We can easily conceive of hundreds of events running counter to the laws of nature; but do these whimsical and absurd conceptions bring the things conceived within the range of possibility? No more than the equally whimsical and absurd conception of the non-existence of matter would bring that conception within the same range.

The necessary existence of matter, then—for all that the doctor has done to it—rests precisely where it was. It had long ago been received as an indisputable doctrine, if not an axiom in philosophy, that out of nothing, no thing can come; and it has never yet been shown to be essentially incorrect. If, therefore, theologians do not relish this doctrine,—if, in their eyes, it looks horrible and grim,—they might surely be at the trouble of showing that something *can* be made from nothing, and nothing from something, instead of resorting to a sly method of getting rid of it by a side-wind. We must agree with Clarke, that something must have existed from eternity; but the question is, what is this something? Whether is it matter of whose existence everything testifies in the strongest, the most irresistible manner; or is it an aggregate of imaginary perfections, physical as well as moral, without a body for their habitation or a medium for their existence? Whether is it something whose existence is a matter of knowledge, a matter of absolute certainty, or something of whose existence we know nothing whatever, but is, on the contrary, the very thing in question?

The necessary existence of anything,—any being, I mean, such as matter is, and God is said to be,—is its self-existence; and to prove it to be self-existent, it is only incumbent to shew cause why it should be uncreated and eternal. Now this has already been done as far as a negative view of the question regarding matter makes admissible. Another view of it is, that matter is the thing above all others absolutely necessary to figure, motion, agency, colour, and what not; that it is the *sine qua non* of our own existence and that of all things else, even the stupendous fabric of the universe itself. Take away matter, and you effect the taking off of every thing of which we can form the slightest idea. All is annihilated except space and duration. Our observations on these, however, we must reserve till we come to notice the more direct treatment of them in Mr Gillespie's argument.

To close this rather tedious part of the discussion, the question of the self-existence of matter may be put in this form.—Either it is eternal, or it is not.—If eternal, it is by consequence self-existent. If not eternal, it must owe its existence to some cause. But to fall upon the latter alternative is clearly to beg the question. It is, as is done in the argument from final causes, to take for granted the prior existence of an agent capable of producing the effect. The existence of such an agent, therefore, ought to be fully demonstrated before the self-existence of matter can legitimately be questioned at all.

CHAP. III.

Fallacies of Dr Clarke—continued.

DR CLARKE's fourth proposition is, " *What the substance or essence of that being which is self-existent or necessarily existing is, we have no idea ; neither is it at all possible for us to comprehend it.*"

That we can have no knowledge whatever of the deified something which Dr Clarke had here in his eye,—either as to essence, substance, or anything else, I most readily and most potently believe. That this should be acknowledged by a materialist, is nothing strange. But strange it certainly is— nay, passing strange ; it surely is ridiculous that the people who so stoutly assert the being of a god, and would thrust their mystical dogmas down our throat—it is surely absurd that these very people, for all their clamour of demonstration,—should be reduced to the miserable necessity of acknowledging that they don't know what it is that they talk about.

What would Dr Clarke himself have said of a person who pretended to prove the existence of a something, till then unknown in nature, but who could tell nothing about its essence,—who could not tell whether it was an animal, a mineral, a vegetable ;—whether it was a solid substance, a liquid, a gas, or whether it possessed gravity and extension ; —and yet gravely declared, that it was impossible ever to find out anything of this kind about it ? This, it is true, is to take a practical view of the case,—and although the latter is certainly the most eligible way of judging of all such matters, we can afford to give the theologian the advantage of any sort of argument he may choose to adopt, however inapplicable to the purpose. What, then, does this concession make for the theologian in the present instance ? Absolutely nothing. If the theological demonstration were thoroughly correct, it ought not only to affect the existence, but every part of the character of deity ;—his essence, his nature, and all his modes of being. Nay, this very knowledge of his nature ought to enable us—by means of certain definitions, axioms, and canons—to predict, with the utmost exactitude, every event in futurity. By the use of points, straight and curve lines, &c., we describe (let us say) an equilateral triangle : but when the description is finished, we perceive properties in the figure which enable us to demonstrate its relations to other species of the triangle, the quadrangle, the circle, sexagon, sphere, cone, and I know not what all else. Now, if a priori reasoning were as available for theological as mathematical purposes, the character and essence of the thing demonstrated ought to be equally comprehended by all who understand the terms in which the demonstration is made, and in any way capable of appreciating the results.—But, alas ! the essence, the nature, and mode of action of the god of our theologues are as yet an enigma, and I fear will for ever remain so, notwithstanding all their demonstrations respecting him.

Dr Clarke tries to get out of the difficulty in which he here finds himself, by comparing the conduct of the unbeliever in denying the existence of a god, to that of a blind or deaf man in denying the existence of colours or sounds. In this comparison he commends the latter as infinitely more reasonable than the former; for the blind or deaf man, he says, can have nothing but testimony for his belief respecting sounds or colours, whereas the atheist, with the least use of his reason, may have " undeniable demonstration" (was there ever any other sort?) for the existence of a supreme being. Although, however, it were admitted that people deficient of any of the external senses, had no other evidence than testimony for the existence of the objects perceived by others through the medium of those senses, the comparison would be altogether invalid. Upon what authority do we inform a blind man of the existence of colours? Is it not upon the authority of evidence which it is not possible he can either perceive or understand? Does the theist, then,

D

possess similar advantages over the athiest? Is he favored with the possession of a sixth or a seventh sense, whereby he can perceive supernatural things,—a race of new existences, with all their associations,—while we remain necessarily and irremediably excluded from so noble and enviable a kind of perception? If so, what is that sense, and how is it exercised? Although we may be unable completely to understand a description of it, or fully to appreciate its benefits, yet it would surely be but an act of charity to make us aware of the helplessness of our condition. If not, why throw a slur upon unbelief as though it were as palpable a perversity as it is said to be for a blind man to deny the existence of colours or a deaf one of sounds? Our possession of those senses of which such unfortunates are destitute, we can easily prove to them by a much stronger sort of evidence than testimony. Let the religious do the same with us, and we shall bow to their authority.—The fact of the case is, that those who presume to teach, are at least equally blind with those they would instruct; equally ignorant with those over whom they would assume such a wonderful superiority.

As a sort of salvo for the awkwardness of maintaining the existence of a thing, of the modes of which he knows nothing, the author makes a false statement respecting our ignorance of all other things. " There is not," he says, " so mean and contemptible a plant or animal, that does not confound the most enlarged understanding upon earth; nay, even the simplest and plainest of all inanimate beings have their essence or substance hidden from us in the deepest and most impenetrable obscurity." Now, what does he mean by a plant or animal confounding the most enlarged understanding on earth? Does he refer to their essence or substance? In that case, we may reply, that none but the worst informed are ignorant of the constituent principles entering into combination in the substance of all animal as well as of vegetable bodies. If it be asked what the essence of these principles is, of carbon for instance, or any of the fifty or sixty substances accounted simple in the present state of chemical science,—I would reply, that the question is impertinent. If the term essence, or substance, bears reference to anything beyond the simple elements of matter, I confess that I do not understand its signification, and would be glad to see it defined. Were water to be resolved into constituents more simple than oxygen and hydrogen, and names referred to such, it would, I dare say, be still inquired, what is the essence of these? But let those who carp and cavil about essence in this manner (having a more occult reference in their eye than to the ultimate principles of things) tell us their meaning, and we shall endeavour to meet their most searching inquiries upon the subject.

Taking matter to be the self-existent being, the converse of Dr Clarke's fourth proposition is thus fairly made out;—namely, that of its essential principles we certainly have *some* idea. But, at all events, give us something half so satisfactory respecting the essence, or substance, or mode of the existence of a god, and we shall be perfectly content. The very fact of speaking of plants and animals, is a proof that we know something of the modifications of matter;—can we say as much for those of deity? The very proposition under notice settles this question.

The fifth proposition is, that " *The self-existent being must be eternal,*"—that is, (not that it has existed from eternity, for that has already been proved, but) that it must continue for ever in existence. This proposition is but very lamely supported. As there is no occasion, however, to deny that the self-existent being—whatever it may be—is eternal, we need not be at the trouble of shewing the misapplication of the author's reasoning.

Dr Clarke's sixth proposition, viz. " That *the self-existent being must be infinite and omnipotent,*" rests entirely, as his third does, upon a view of *Necessity,* which has already been shewn to be both partial and unphilosophical. It is only requisite to observe here, that the argument brought in proof of the proposition is exceedingly defective. It is shortly this;—" because something must of necessity be self-existent, therefore it is necessary that it must likewise be infinite." Now, although it be indisputable that *something* must be eternal, as it also is, that *something* must be infinite : the something in the one case is not proved to be identical with the something in the other ; and as it does not at all follow, by consequence, the argument amounts to nothing. To recur to fact, matter may be regarded as eternal and space infinite. We must, it is true, award both attributes to the latter; but, at same time, we cannot deny to the former that which is ascribed to it. Matter, indeed, may be infinite as well as self-existent; but if so, it is not because there exists between these qualities anything like an indissoluble relation.

Having, in his own estimation, proved the omnipresence of the something which has existed from eternity, the author hence infers that it " must be a most simple, unchangeable, uncorruptible being; *without parts, figure, motion, divisibility,* or any other such properties as we find in matter." And wherefore? Because " all these things do plainly and necessarily imply finiteness in their very notion, and are utterly inconsistent with complete infinity." This doctrine may be essential to a being made up of a heap of abstractions, but certainly sounds very strangely when applied to a being such as every god is represented. Even Dr Clarke himself speaks of his god as a male person, possessed of certain powers and moral attributes. If therefore his own language does not imply finity, I cannot conceive what does. Does not personality imply finiteness? does not agency imply the same thing? But it is endless to follow out this contemptible reasoning. It is inconsistent and contradictory, as well as absurd.

The 7th proposition is, " *That the self-existent being can be but one.*" " To suppose two or more distinct beings (it is argued) existing of themselves necessarily and independent of each other, implies this plain contradiction; that each of them being independent of the other, they may, either of them, be supposed to exist alone, so that it will be no contradiction to imagine the other not to exist, and consequently neither of them will be necessarily existing." Here again, as in his reasoning upon the third proposition, the reverend author places his whole dependence on mathematical *Neces-sity*. But bearing in mind the evident worthlessness of such dependence, I would only observe, that it is with the real state-of things we have to do, and not with mathematical contradictions at all. If matter, for instance, as a whole, be not allowed to be unique, it follows, from our previous evi-dence of its eternity, that there must be at least a plurality of self-existent beings. Even although the unity of matter were granted, if we are to call space a being, the same con-clusion appears to be unavoidable. Unless, indeed, space and duration, and the diversity of matter, are to be excluded from view (which would be incompatible with a priori prin-ciples), this seventh proposition must for ever remain unte-nable upon any reasonable grounds.

Dr Clarke's argument a priori stops here. In his eighth proposition, and those following, he had to prove that the self-existent being must be intelligent, and all-powerful, and a free-agent, and wise, and good, and just, and so forth. But this the author clearly perceived could not be made out a priori. What, therefore, was to be done? He had set out with undertaking to *demonstrate* the being and attributes of god, and the task could not, of course, be performed with-out intelligence and all the rest of it sharing in the demon-stration;—how, then, was he to proceed?—Even by being contented with following the humble course of reasoning consequentially instead of necessarily. He begins by carry-ing matters with a high hand; by attempting to make out every thing a flat mathematical contradiction that does not quadrate with his preconceived theory: he ends by recur-ring to the apologetic mode of argument adopted by others many hundred years before! And what does the doctor make of all his shifts,—of all his turns to catch the cur-rent as it serves, whatever point the wind may be blowing from? Nothing at all to boast of: nothing even capable of serving as a consolation for having been forced to so hum-bling a step, for having employed so crooked and inconsis-tent a policy.

The two arguments of our author, in fact, counteract

each other. If the first be well-founded, the second cannot; and if the second be well-founded, the first cannot. Suppose he had established the whole of the propositions up to the seventh inclusive, we have only a something eternal, independent, unchangeable, unique, incomprehensible, and everywhere present; whose nonexistence, whose temporality, whose dependency, and so forth, cannot be conceived: a something, in short, that answers to our notions of space; —does that establish the existence of a deity? Are we to call space not merely a being but a god? To settle this question, we may ask, what are the divine attributes? Are they not, according to the author's own description, an assemblage of all possible perfections, and that, too, if the expression be allowable, in an infinite degree? Can we, then, ascribe infinite intelligence, or *any* intelligence, to such a something? Can we ascribe to it infinite power, or any power at all? Can we ascribe agency, whether free or not free, to that which is immoveable—to that which even excludes from the consideration of it the conception of motion altogether? Dr Clarke himself has declared this to be impossible. What, then, does the demonstration amount to? The existence of a mere nonentity.

On the other hand, taking the author's own absolute necessity as the basis of all sound demonstration, and the criterion by which we are to try all that assumes this character,—what does he make of the intelligence, and wisdom, and goodness, and power of God? He does not so much as pretend that these are necessary to the Something whose existence he has demonstrated.—The conclusion, therefore, to which we are necessarily driven, is,—either that his necessity is good for nothing in the argument—in which case his whole demonstration falls to the ground—or that it leaves the god of that demonstration without power, without intelligence, justice, goodness, truth!!!

CHAP. IV.

Fallacies of Mr Richard Jack.

IT would be a fearful task to toil through the dreary wanderings of this ungainly author. In perusing his work, one would imagine he had been born with theorems in his head, and a rule and compasses in his hands;—and were it not that he himself tells us of certain misfortunes which befel him on his flight from the Scottish capital, and its rebel occupiers, in the memorable year forty-five, we should scarcely have thought him susceptible of human passions, or capable of taking a share in the concerns of those stirring times. His performance is entitled, " Mathematical Principles of Theology; or, the Existence of God geometrically demonstrated, in three books." (*London,* 1747. *8vo. pp.* 328.)—Perhaps I ought not to notice the work at all: it is of a character so prosing, formal, and roundabout. The tactician draws his lines of circumvallation at so great a distance from the fortress he purposes to reduce ; his approaches are made so tardily, and with so little energy, that we are apt to lose patience at his over-precaution, and waste of pains as well as time. If all this were a sure precursor of success, we should have nothing to complain of; but even his closing positions are so ill chosen, as either to be perfectly harmless, or to lie entirely at the mercy of the enemy. The book is, nevertheless, a great curiosity. It furnishes the finest specimens anywhere to be found, of strict mathematical reasoning as applied to theology. It may therefore be amusing, if not instructive, to touch upon a few of the author's happiest efforts (and those upon the most important points of the discussion,) were it only to show the effect even of the purest logic, when pressed into the service of the argument a priori for the being and attributes of a god.

The first book, consisting of forty-five propositions and

theorems, is taken up in proving the self-existence of an independent being. In the second, an attempt is made to demonstrate that that being cannot be matter; for all vision-aries must have a fling at this untractable impediment to their motions—this desperate eye-sore to all their specula-tions. Mr Jack says, (*prop.* 41, *theor.* 40,)—"Matter is a dependent being, because that being which can have any change or mutation made on any of the powers or properties it possesses, is a dependent being; but a change or mutation can be made on some of the powers or qualities that matter or any material being possesses; therefore matter is a de-pendent being, which was to be demonstrated."—It is to be observed, that a dependent being had been previousiy de-fined, a being whose existence is the effect of some other being; so that this syllogism purports to be a demonstration of matter having been created out of nothing! How is this? By what magic is so rare a case made out? I say at once, by the shallow, paltry trick of equivocation. The subject of the major premiss, which ought to have been identical with the predicate of the definition of a dependent being previously given, is totally different from it. The de-finition, it is true, as applied to matter, involves an impossi-bility. Besides taking for granted the existence of some agent, unknown and undescribed, its power of bringing all material things into existence is asumed. But if the defi-nition in question falls, the conclusion that matter is a de-pendent being, reaches to its forms only, leaving its inde-pendence as to existence untouched.

Well; but this is theological demonstration. Demonstra-tion, certainly, much more easy, and infinitely better adapt-ed to the subject in hand, than the vexatious and trouble-some process of induction; by which we are bound to pro-duce an agent, and prove the extent of its powers and mode of operation—and that too by experience—before we can le-gitimately ascribe to it any effect whatever. Here, nothing further is necessary than to frame a hypothesis—nothing more than to

" Call some spirit from the vasty deep;"

invest it with the attributes in which popular prejudice has arrayed the object of its adoration, and by the flourish of a conjuring wand, bid matter begone into its assumed original nothingness. Mighty magicians! If our reasoners a priori could but tell us where they get the creative power of which they speak so much, independent of the thing they go about to destroy, they would render their argument somewhat more tangible. If they could even tell us of a single change effected in matter by means of their pretended agency, the information would both be new and directly to the point.— But, alas for them! how should they know anything of a being necessarily prior to the existence of the material world,—or (supposing such a being) its essence or *modus operandi?* In any of the numberless changes effected upon material bodies, do we see any thing operating except other bodies of the same kind? Can we even *conceive* of any other than material agency? If aught-else than substance operates in the mutations observed in physical phenomena, Nature, by denying the fact, betrays and belies its god, and science and philosophy are left with a heavy account of heresy to answer for.

After having demolished the self-existence of matter, Mr Jack proceeds to prove that it owes its existence to his own "independent being." As the argument he employs on this occasion affects to demonstrate the intelligence of the thing referred to in the first book, and is the only one which touches-upon this highly momentous point, it is the more worthy of attention. It is as follows :—

. " The self-existent and independent being does possess a self-determining power, or volition, and that self-determining power or volition is the cause of the existence of the first temporary being." (Book II. prop. 32, theor. 31.)

" Let A represent the self-existent and independent being, B the first temporary being: I say, the self-existing and independent being A is possessed of a self-determining power, or volition, and that self-determining power or volition, is the cause of the existence of the first temporary being B. For because the existence of the first temporary being B, is

E

the effect that arises from the exertion of some of the powers or qualities of the self-existing and independent being A, and the cause of the exertion of any power or quality of the self-existing and independent being, is a self-determining power, that the self-existing and independent being does possess; therefore the cause of the exertion of that power or quality of the self-existing and independent being ·A, which does produce the existence of B, is a self-determining power or volition that it does possess, and will be the cause of B's existence; consequently the self-existing and independent being A, does possess a self-determining power or volition, which self-determining power or volition is the cause of the existence of the first temporary being B's existence. Therefore *the self-existing and independent being does possess a self-determining power, which self-determining power is the cause of the existence of the first temporary being,* which was to be demonstrated."

Who can doubt, after so luminous and strictly geometrical a demonstration, that the creation of a mathematician's mind possesses intelligence; that by the simple act of its volition it has called all things into existence? What signifies it, although the latter be assumed as the effect of the former? What, at least, does it signify, that the introduction of one of the factors into the theorem is gratuitous? Surely no one can expect that so trivial an affair as the creation of a temporary being by a self-existent one should be proved. Do we not see that that fact is brought in as a proof of the self-determining power of A, and that this power is next made out, in the clearest manner, to be the cause of the existence of B? What more than this beautiful circle of reasoning does the captious infidel want? Descartes boastfully exclaimed, in the style of Archimedes,—" Give me matter and motion, and I will make you a universe;" but, with much scantier materials, our new-fangled theorists perform a great deal more,—only give them A and B, and they produce you both the universe and its creator!

The greatest part of Mr. Jack's theorems, problems, &c. &c. consisting of upwards of an hundred in number, is

substance, is to maintain there is no eternal substance."—
Now, with reference to matter, this doctrine appears to be
at variance with fact. No one, it is true, can logically maintain that matter is *not* infinitely extended; because that procedure would be to engage in the proof of an absolutely
negative position, which it is impossible to establish. At the
same time it cannot be denied, that it would be a very hard
task to bring sufficient evidence in support of a contrary
affirmation: we cannot prove that it *is* infinitely extended.
The fact is, we cannot say whether matter be infinitely extended or not. In so far as our experience goes, and our
observation can carry us, we find substance completely occupying every part of space. This shall be shown when we
come to review Mr Gillespie's notions relative to the divisibility of matter. We see worlds on worlds and systems
upon systems, floating around us in all directions, accompa-
nied by such circumstances as to prove the presence of matter to the utmost distance which the best telescopes can
reach. But what, after all, is the greatest latitude we can
allow to such distance compared with immensity? Judging
from analogy, indeed, we might be ready to conclude even
the infinity of space to be filled with some substance or
other. Analogical reasoning, however, is necessarily false,
consisting, as it does, of applying to one thing the deductions
of our experience respecting another. It is grossly unphilosophical, therefore, to build any theory or any argument
upon it.

Although it be frankly admitted, then, that we neither
have, nor can have, any knowledge of the infinity of material
extension, more than we can have of its limits; that does
not at all involve a denial of the eternity of matter. We
perceive a vast universe in existence, but were it only a single atom of matter, no power of man could reduce it to annihilation, or even conceive of a power capable of producing
this effect. To suppose, therefore, that matter ever began
to exist, or to suppose its existence capable of termination,
is to admit the occurrence of these stupendous effects without
a cause. This absurdity can only be avoided by assuming

the existence of some immaterial being acting as an agent in the case,—which assumption is a double, if not a threefold absurdity. For, first, we have to take for granted the existence of what is inconceivable, namely, an immaterial being: or else that of some substance exempted, and without any reason, from the essential laws of its nature. Next have we to endue the supposed being with power sufficient to accomplish (and mark what it is that is to be accomplished) the creation or annihilation of matter,—either of which is an impossibility.

CHAP. VI.

Fallacies of Mr Gillespie—The " Argument."

This grand argument is laid out in two books. In the first, the metaphysico-theologian endeavours to prove that some being exists which is the *sine qua non* of every other thing in existence. It consists of three parts, or series of propositions, maintaining, first, that Space is this being; second, that Duration is also a being of the same kind; and, third, that these are not different, but identical. The second book ascribes to the subject of the forementioned proofs, the divine attributes of omnipresence, unlimited power, and freedom of agency.

We cannot afford time—much less can it be expected that others should afford patience—both to make a general analysis of this argument, and examine the reasonings brought up in support of the different parts of it. As, therefore, authors are peculiarly jealous of their privileges, and tetchy and froward with regard to any freedom used in the treatment of their expressions, we shall take the most laborious, and, at the same time, least advantageous way of combating Mr Gillespie's principles,—book by book, and proposition by proposition. This course is the more necessary, as the argument a priori, unlike that derived from experience, depends upon a chain of reasoning,—not upon the pointed putting of a single case, or the tautological repetition of a thousand.

The first proposition,—*"Infinity of extension is necessarily existing,"*—it would be absurd in the extreme to deny. No more can we imagine any limit prescribable to extension, than we can imagine the outside of a house to be in the inside of it. The same unqualified assent, however, cannot be accorded to proposition the second; namely, that *"Infinity of extension is necessarily indivisible."*

Here, the author has given up his abstract necessity, and looks for something like experiment as alone capable of satisfying him: for, notwithstanding some unmeaning talk, intended to explain away this desertion of his own principles, he evidently insists upon a real division—an actual separation of parts, with some distance, however little between them, as that which he means by divisibility. If Mr Gillespie pleads not guilty to this charge, I would ask him how mathematicians have always regarded the smallest particle of matter divisible to infinity? Do they ever contemplate actual separation of parts in such cases? No; but parts—as Mr. Gillespie himself has it—in the sense of partial consideration only. When they speak of the hemispheres of the earth, divided either by the plane of the equator, or that passing from the meridian of Greenwich to the 180th degree of longitude,—are they necessarily guilty of speaking unintelligibly? If not, how is it that extension is necessarily indivisible?

It may be said, perhaps, that although matter is, mentally, easy enough to divide, it is impossible to apply the same process to extension. But is not the space occupied by the earth,—or say, its useful little representation, a twelve or a twenty-inch globe,—as easily conceived to be divisible by a mathematical plane, as the globe itself, which is not really, but only mentally divided? A mathematical point has no dimensions, because whatever possesses dimensions must possess figure, and that which has figure cannot be a point. In like manner, a plane cannot have thickness, since whatever

F

is of the smallest thickness is not a plane but a solid. In dividing space by abstraction, therefore, there is no *necessity*, as our author would have us believe, of falling into the absurdity of space divided by actual separation of the parts, leaving no space between them.

It would be of no great consequence although the second proposition were as irrefragable as the first; for it bears upon nothing at all applicable to any being, whether real or imaginary. But we need not always allow even gratuitous fallacies to escape. The exposure, at least, shows the badness of the cause that renders the adoption of them necessary. If Mr Gillespie's indivisibility be understood in an abstract sense, his proposition is not true; if, in reference to actual experiment, he may be applauded for having recourse to inductive instead of a priori reasoning, he need not so soon have neglected the principles upon which he started, without intimating some ground for the change.

A corollary is here introduced, asserting the immoveability of extension. It is true, that either finity or infinity of extension can never be supposed capable of motion. Space cannot be carried out of itself, nor can those parts of it occupied by Mont Blanc, for example, and the Peak of Teneriffe, ever be imagined to change places. To the truth of what is here maintained, therefore, we must give unreserved assent, independent of its nominal connection with the false doctrine immediately going before.

But we now come to a proposition which may be said to carry with it all the strength, if it has any, as well as the weakness, of Mr Gillespie's " Argument." It is the third in number, and announces that " *There is necessarily a* BEING *of infinity of extension.*"

If we had not already seen that the author's reasoning leads us to conclude that his Being is to be regarded as something substantial, we should have been at a loss what to make of the subject of the above predicate. As a logician would say, it is not distributed. But if we refer to the third division of his introduction, we find him contending that the necessary being must be of the character now ascribed to that subject. At the twenty-third section he avows that " It may be laid down as one of those truths which admit of no contradiction, that with regard to the uncreated substance, at least, virtue (meaning power, I presume,) cannot be without substance. Speaking of this substance," the author goes on to say, " Sir Isaac Newton hath these words,"—which may be rendered—" Omnipresence is not by power alone, but also by substance; for *without substance, power cannot possibly subsist*."

Not only, however, is the necessary being of Mr Gillespie said to be a substance, and therefore by his own and Sir Isaac Newton's showing, possessed of virtue or power, but it has already been designated, " the intelligent cause of all things." I am quite aware, that neither intelligence nor power can be demonstrated of any thing a priori, which we shall see when this author's reasoning upon those attributes fall in our way. We may, nevertheless, in endeavouring to bear in mind the description of Being, of whom so great things are predicated, avail ourselves of any expression of opinion respecting it, that may be scattered throughout the work. It is only on this account that I have at present alluded to these after-considerations at all.

Relative to a Being of this sort, then,—at all events, relative to a substantial being, the truth of the predicate is what we have now to try. The evidence in support of the third proposition is stated in the form of a dilemma. " Either infinity of extension subsists, or, (which is the same thing,) we conceive it to subsist, without a support or substratum ; or, it subsists not, or we conceive it not to subsist, without a support or substratum. First, If infinity of extension subsist without a substratum, then it is a substance.—Secondly, If infinity of extension subsist not without a substratum, then, it being a contradiction to deny there is infinity of extension, it is a contradiction to deny there is a substratum to it."

The conclusion deduced from the latter alternative, besides appearing lame and impotent, is somewhat laughable. But allowing its logic to pass, it may be worth while, if only for amusement, to try the force of this, the negative horn of the dilemma, by ascertaining what it is made of.—The primary signification of the word substratum is, a thing lying under something else. Supposing, for instance, a bed of gravel to lie under the soil, gravel is the substratum of that soil; if there be sandstone below that, the sandstone is the substratum of the gravel; if coal be found beneath the rock, coal is the substratum of it, and so on as far as we can penetrate. To say, therefore, that space must have a substratum, is nothing less than saying that it must have something to rest upon; something to hold it up. That is,—Space must have limits; and there must be something in existence beyond its limits to keep it from falling—out of itself! If this be not the acme of absurdity, a ship falling overboard, as our sailors' jest goes, is no longer a joke; and the clown who boasted that he could swallow himself, boasted of nothing that he might not be reasonably be expected to perform.

Should it be contended that the term ought to be understood in its secondary acceptation, and that the substratum of the infinity of extension subsists within itself, as any material body is said to be the substratum of its own extension:—I would remark, that we know of nothing possessing extension except matter,—nothing else that can stand as an object to which extension may be ascribed as a property; and that matter, not existing by mathematical, but only by physical necessity, cannot be the substratum referred to. Hence it is evident that, in material bodies, comprising all that we *do* know, or *can* know of Being, it is impossible to find anything that will serve Mr Gillespie's purpose. Even this impossibility overlooked, however, what is it that next meets our view?—One substance occupying infinite extension, and another occupying part of this extension, if not also the whole of it; in other words, two things at the same time occupying the same space. Theology always entangles its advocates in inextricable absurdities.

A religious friend who has corresponded with me upon this point, alleges that the substance of the substratum of infinite extension is not material ; but this is mere babble; something he has been taught to repeat,—not the dictate of his sounder judgment. Substance and matter are the same. The words are synonymous and convertible. When used otherwise they become unintelligible ; inasmuch as we might then talk of an unsubstantial substance and immaterial matter.

But, to refer to the first proposition,—has it not been demonstrated that infinity of extension exists necessarily ?— that it exists, *per se,* by the most abstract and metaphysical necessity ? In what sort of predicament, then, must that reasoning appear, which gives up a leading and universally admitted truth by placing it in a questionable position ? Mr Gillespie's dilemma recognises, at least, the possibility of infinite extension requiring a substratum to support it—infinite extension, which is itself necessary ! How is this ? Was it found that although space possessed a few of the divine attributes, it did not possess all, nor anything like all that were deemed needful to constitute a respectable deity ? Notwithstanding appearances, I should hope not. But, at any rate, we are again landed in a quagmire of absurdity—the absurdity of supposing a thing to be dependent and independent at the same time. If space must be conceived a priori necessary, to talk of a substratum being necessary in the same sense of the word is nonsense : on the other hand, if it stands in need of a substratum, the foundation stone of this great argument must crumble into dust, and be unfit to serve as a substratum to anything.

But if we are dissatisfied with the author's substratum, we are not much better situated with the alternative left us ; for according to the dilemma he has imposed upon us, we are obliged to conclude that infinity of existence is itself a substance. I had thought infinity a mere nominal adjunct allowed to space, from the circumstance of our being unable to conceive limits to its extent; but the theist, it seems, thinks otherwise. Infinity, with him, must be a substance. On the same ground, we might contend that finity is a substance too. Supposing, however, that space infinitely extended is what he means, all that we can say is, that if it be a substance it is no longer space, or extension, or any thing else than,—just a substance;—unless it may be both extension and substance at the same moment. But these are profane thoughts. Perhaps according to the new school of theology, not only may a book be a substance, but its extension may also be a substance, its weight another, its colour a third, and so forth. Let us hear, however, how the divine theory of infinity of extension being a substance is to be sustained.—Mark with what boldness of reasoning it is brought out. The infidel must look well to his footing and points of defence, lest he be laid prostrate by its overwhelming force.

" If any one should deny that it is a substance, it so subsisting;" (that is, without a support or substratum,) "to prove beyond contradiction the utter absurdity of such denial, we have but to defy him to show why infinity of extension is not a substance, so far forth as it can subsist by itself or without a substratum."

A new era has thus dawned upon logic. A grand discovery is on the eve of rendering her power irresistible, and her reign everlasting and glorious. It is to be henceforth no longer necessary for us to prove an affirmative : assert what we may, no one dare deny our assertions. For to prove beyond contradiction the utter absurdity of such denial, we have only to put a brave face on it, and throw a defiance in the teeth of our opponent to prove the negative.

But waiving, in the meantime, our plea of want of evidence for the affirmative, a simple man would say in relation to the case before us, that substance possesses attraction, which extension does not ; that it is observed under a thousand varieties of figure, density, colour, motion, taste, odour, combustion, crystalization, &c. which neither extension nor infinity ever is, or can in its nature be. He might, in his deplorable ignorance, ask if ever infinity was weighed, or extension analyzed and its elements reduced to gas? This would, I dare say, only evince in the eyes of the theologian, that such a person had no idea of the very conveni-

ent art of applying metaphysical language to things physical; whereby a mere abstraction, or at most a property of
something else, can so easily be charmed into a reality. His
showing why infinity of extension is not a substance, therefore, would be set down as grovelling and common-place,
and, by consequence, useless.

After all, however, how does the notable proposition
stand, that there is necessarily a Being of infinity of extension? The principle of the argument brought up in support
of it—the dilemma, in short—gives way on every side. It
stands without a vestige of backing, except from the vain
and swelling words of a blustering defiance, the value of
which no one but a fool could be at a loss to estimate.

The author himself, indeed, seems not half sure of having
made good the doctrine he has announced: for after having
done all he could do, by the foisting in of a substratum
upon extension to the destruction of its necessary existence,
—he comforts himself with the reflection, that it is of very
little consequence whether men will or will not consent to
call this substratum by the name of being or substance, because "'tis certain that the word substance or being, has never
been employed, can never be employed, to stand for anything more, at least, than the substratum of infinity of extension." It is, of course, of no manner of importance whether
men consent to do what they always have done and must
continue to do, or whether they will not. But how far is the
because and its certainty consistent with the lurking suspi-
cion of the honoured name of Being or substance being
refused to his unsupported substratum? Yet, on the very
heels of this misgiving, he concludes,—"There is, *then*, NE-
CESSARILY, a Being of infinity of extension." The worthy
old father of the church, who declared his belief of a christian dogma because it was impossible, is not far from having
a logician of the mathematical school to keep him in coun-
tenance. Mr Gillespie frames a most absolute conclusion
with his premises dubiously faltering on his lips.

CHAP. VII.

Fallacies of Mr Gillespie—The " Argument" continued.

THE fourth proposition of this argument—that " the being
of infinity of extension is necessarily of unity and simplicity"
—is founded upon the baseless fabric of extension being
indivisible; of its being in itself a substance, or requiring a
substratum to support it. There is a scholium attached to
it, however, which we must not entirely lose sight of. It is
levelled against the unity and simplicity, and by consequence
(as the author thinks) the infinity of the material universe.
It is not that I conceive the conclusion of this scholium essential to a right view of the eternity of matter, or even the
question of the existence of a god, far less that the premises are so, that I make any observations upon either.
The self-existence of matter stands high above the reach of
the argument a priori; but it is surely more direct and proper to expose the weakness of that argument, than allow it
to retain a reputation for close and rigid-reasoning which it
does not at all merit. In the present instance, as in all
others, there is not a single position taken in hostility to antitheistical principles, that will not also be found hostile,
either to physical science or sound philosophy.

To be the substratum of the infinity of extension, is held
to be indispensible in the self-existent substance. This is
the principle here adopted; but in reply to a similar theory
in Dr Clarke's " Demonstration," it has been shown to be contrary to reason and the nature of things. Upon that point,
therefore, we are not now going to contend. It is upon the
doctrine of matter being finite in extension.

" To put to the proof," says Mr Gillespie, " whether or
not the material universe can be such substratum, we have
but to ask, are the parts of the material universe divisible

from each other? and are they moveable among themselves?—for if they be so divisible, if so moveable, then the material universe cannot be the substratum of infinity of extension."

That matter is divisible, (on a certain and special construction of terms,) no one will deny; but that it is absolutely so, is not true. We can divide substance by abstraction as we divide space. If it be of any specific body we speak, we can, in reality, separate one part from another. This, however, is not absolutely to divide matter. In the discussion of his second proposition, the author makes manifest the absurdity of supposing space really divisible, since that would be to suppose the parts separated without having any space between them. Now, in the same sense of divisibility, matter is not more subject to it than space. I grant that we may conceive of an absolute separation of substance generally, which we cannot do in the case of extension. But that is not the question. It is real and generic separation we have in view. The houses on opposite sides of a street stand separate; is that to say, however, that there is no substance between them? Is it not childish to suppose, that by cutting an apple in two, we have actually divided matter so as to leave nothing of a material kind between the parts of the fruit? It is quite common to say, a bottle is empty, after the liquor it contained has been poured out; and this may be a convenient enough way of expressing ourselves when we have little else than eatables and drinkables to talk of; but is a vessel in this case really empty? is it completely exhausted of all kind of substance?

But we may as well go into the hypothesis of a vacuum at once, for to this point the argument obviously tends. What, then, is a vacuum? It is space, I presume, without any matter being present at all. Is such a state of things, however, anywhere to be found? I think not, and that it does not appear possible to find it. What is commonly called a vacuum, is only a part of space, say the interior of a receiver deprived, in a great measure, of atmospheric air. The extraction of the atmosphere, be it observed, is never

G

completely effected. In the use of the pneumatic pump, each succeeding stroke only brings off a certain proportion of what the receiver contains—say one-half—so that the residue being never more than half taken away, the most constant application of the best constructed machine can never make the exclusion of the air perfect. Even in the Torricellian operation, the alleged perfection of the vacuum depends upon the crude notion of there being neither air nor pores in the fluid by which it is formed, which is not the fact. Yet, after all, supposing the air entirely shut out, is there no other species of matter left behind? Where is light, and where heat? As light, however, may be excluded to a considerable extent, I would only ask whether heat be a substance or only a property of substance? Taking the thing at the worst, the presence of heat indicates, of course, the presence of some substance, of which it is, in such instance, a property. This conclusion is inevitable, unless a quality of a thing may be present, where the thing itself is not. It must here be remembered, that the greatest degree of cold ever experienced, only indicates a lower degree of heat than had previously been known—not that it is impossible for the amount of heat to be further reduced.

Should it be demanded—as it is always commendable to do on such occasions—what the substance is which we deem to be present in what is usually denominated a vacuum,—we may reply—the electric fluid. No substance is capable of excluding it. As water seeks its level, the fluid in question presses everywhere, that it may be everywhere present; and with this tendency, it penetrates, in a manner the most irresistible, every thing that can be opposed to its course.

The notion of there being a vacuum in nature, is as idle as the attempt to prove one by artificial means. The demonstration cannot, in any case, succeed. Some of our astronomers, particularly of the Newtonian sect, were obliged in a manner to adopt this doctrine, in order to back out their theological assumptions. They supposed the planets to have been hurled from the hand of a god, like bowls by a gamester, and that no new impetus of a supernatural kind being

observed, the motion of these vast bodies must be perpetu-
ally retarded, unless a perfect vacuum had been wisely pro-
vided for them to revolve in. But the dogma is now scattered to the winds. The single phenomenon of comets
describing, at each successive revolution, progressively
diminished orbits, settles the point. Were there no substance present to resist their motion, we must conclude, upon
the principles of the truly great Newton, that the centrifugal
force would necessarily and for ever counterbalance the
attractive.

There is, however, more extensive evidence than this.
Among the sublime discoveries which have rendered the
name of Herschel illustrious, none is more sadly interesting,
than that of a prevailing tendency to contraction observed in
the multitudinous systems of the universe. In the nebulæ—
in the Magellanic clouds—and even the milky way, the same
unceasing compression is observed, and of course the
same evidence is offered of the presence of a resisting medium.

The contemplation of this probable, though remote con-
summation of all existing relations, may excuse a remark or
two relative to an infinite series of beings. If secondary
planets are ultimately destined to fall in upon their primaries,
and these together upon the central bodies to which they are
subordinate, changes upon a vast scale must result, and new
formations follow. The laws occasioning these changes,
acting eternally, must be the source of eternal revolutions.
Where, then, in these circumstances, are we to look for a
beginning? In the most unceasing endeavours we may
make to reach the starting point of nature's operations, we
shall find our labours vain ; and every attempt of this sort
as completely foiled as in seeking for their end.

Although, however, we were fully warranted in rejecting
the system of change which brought along with it these
gloomy forebodings, of all the greatness and glory of man
being sunk in everlasting forgetfulness—although it were
argued, and that successfully, that the deductions made from
the data stated regarding the ethereal fluid are yet undeter-

mined,—we are not left without ample grounds, in as far as our researches reach, for holding the doctrine of a plenum. Wherever we turn our eyes, we observe matter in existence. Beyond the sphere of human observation we know nothing. If science cannot demonstrate that matter is infinite in extension, much less can Mr Gillespie demonstrate that it is not so. His conclusion, therefore, falls to the ground.

I need say little, I dare say, respecting the argument derived from the motion of material bodies: it amounts to nothing. The different parts of matter only change places; unless, therefore, substance lose its extension, — nay, its very existence—by being moved, there can be no foundation for detracting from its extension, finite or infinite, on that account.

I have thus gone more fully than I intended, or even anticipated, into an examination of the scholium to Mr Gillespie's fourth proposition. The sum and substance of it is this—(and indeed it is but a contemptible fallacy)—Because matter does not agree in character and properties with a mere abstraction,—that is, because it is not what it is not—it cannot be the substratum of infinite extension; it cannot be the *sine qua non* of all things; it cannot be the self-existent being!

Upon the fifth and last proposition of this part of the work, that "there is necessarily but *one* being of infinity of expansion," it is hardly worth our pains to remark. The existence of Mr Gillespie's being of infinity of extension having failed under proof, any consideration relative to its supposed exclusiveness of all other necessary existences, cannot be of much avail. Even admitting his substratum of space, however, why may there not be two, or twenty, as well as one? No reason can be assigned why infinity of expansion (which the author now appropriates to space, as he does extension to matter,) should have an *immaterial* something to keep it in existence, that would not prove that that something should have something else to keep it in existence as well.

But it is needless to fight with shadows which may be

raised as fast as they are demolished. They are the illusions of a subtle imagination, fabricated to support what cannot be maintained on fair and tangible grounds. The supposition of a plurality of necessary beings, against which our theorist so strongly inveighs, springs from his own theogonal geology. This spurious, this imaginary sort of science, should either not have been resorted to, or no objection should be taken to its inevitable consequences.

CHAP. VIII.

False Reasoning of Mr Gillespie ; Second Part of his Work.

THE second part of the work before us, approaches as near as possible to similarity with the first. " Infinity of duration is necessarily existing; infinity of duration is necessarily indivisible; infinity of duration is necessarily immoveable; there is necessarily a *being* of infinity of duration : the being of infinity of duration is necessarily of unity and simplicity; there is necessarily but *one* being of infinity of duration."— These are the propositions—these the dogmas that are now brought forward for discussion. And wherein do they differ from those already examined and exploded? In nothing but the substitution of infinity of duration for that of extension. The same process is repeated; the same reasoning gone through, almost to the very letter.

It may have been necessary, from the method of demonstration adopted, to come over the same ground and reiterate the same deductions on the slightest alteration in the subject of proof. As in mathematical affairs the validity of the argument a priori may depend upon the minuteness and accuracy of detail, regardless of the repulsiveness of a slavish tautology. There is no reason, however, why we should follow so uninviting an example. It will be sufficient to show that the refutation of the doctrines sought to be established in the former case, applies with equal force to those propounded in the latter.

To effect this application cannot be hard to accomplish. If, indeed, there be any difference between the author's reasoning in the different parts, it is worse in the second than the first. Although extension may be conceived of as a pure abstraction, it is also conceivable as one of the properties, if not the only indispensible property of matter. But can we entertain any such notion respecting duration? Who ever heard of duration being a property of matter? Upon the hypothesis of substance being infinitely extended, we may regard it as " the substratum of infinity of extension;" at least we understand what is meant by such a circumstance being predicated of substance. But how are we to understand what is meant by anything being the substratum of the infinity of duration? Yet that something is such a substratum is what is broadly declared to be the fact.— This is what we are unhesitatingly required to admit, or else give in to the monstrous proposition, that duration is itself a substance!

If the author will consult " An Analysis of the Phenomena of the Human Mind," published some few years ago by Mr Mill, he will find even the first proposition relative to duration questioned by that philosopher. We cannot indeed suppose duration to have had a commencement, nor imagine a termination for it; but the writer whose name has been mentioned, concludes that the past being already *out* of existence, and the future not being yet *in* existence, there can be no duration in existence at all. To consider the matter thus, is perhaps to consider it too curiously; for whatever is done, even what may require the labour of an age to effect, is done in the successive instants of time as they pass, however minute those instants may be reckoned, and however, as of course they must proportionably be, rapid in their succession. All that I would infer is, that infinity of time, if not more an abstract consideration than infinite space, is at all events fully as much so.

Why then should duration have a substratum or support

for its existence? Why suppose that it cannot exist of itself and independently of all substance? Or, making this supposition, why lay down as a fundamental principle, the absolute and metaphysically necessary existence of infinity of duration? To reconcile these suppositions is essential to the validity of Mr Gillespie's argument; but is there any way of reconciling them? The thing is impossible.

But about duration, or, as the author has it, infinity of duration being a substance—what could have driven him to a hypothesis so outrageously extravagant? Nothing, I am persuaded, but the sheer desperation of a dauntless advocate in a sinking cause. I do not mean that at the present day theism is going down—perhaps it may never go down ; for it is wondrously well borne up by the inflated supports of passion, self-interest, and prejudice, which preserve it from its otherwise certain fate. All I mean is, that casting aside its unworthy, yet popular dependencies, and relying on reason alone,—not the best argument in all the moods and figures of the schools, could keep it from finding the bottom.

If duration were substantial, it would have to be a series of substances, and so resemble the ghosts in Macbeth's vision,—another and another coming into view and passing out in quick succession—till we should be glad to get quit of the phantoms, and exclaim with the tyrant, " I'll see no more." How else should we have any notion of what is indicated by the substance of duration? Can we conceive of a substance to be in existence and out of existence at the same time? If not, we may take leave to ask if the substance of any part of duration already past be yet in being, while according to our vulgar conceptions, unsubstantial duration itself is not? Or can we recal the hours of yesterday, and constantly grow younger instead of growing old?—But it is in vain to attempt reducing the vagaries of a subtle imagination to consistency, or the order of natural relations. Our endeavours not unfrequently involve us in a labyrinth of the theoretical absurdities we would thereby unravel. We might go on, by way of illustration, to suppose motion a substance, —and figure, and colour, and all the rest of it; or to contend that duration was of a particular density, or bore the shape of an aged man with an hour-glass and scythe. The shorter way, however, is to conclude at once, that when duration becomes a substance it ceases to be duration.

In supporting the unity and simplicity of the being of infinite duration, an argument is introduced in scholium first to the fourth proposition, going to show, that *a succession of beings* cannot be the subject of what is there predicated. The reason assigned for this deduction is, that the parts of the succession are divisible from each other, and moveable among themselves. Now, this is what may be called hunting in a wrong scent, or reasoning according to the fallacy logically denominated *ignoratio elenchi ;* for the separation of things from each other, as well as their motions, relate to space, and not to duration at all. If, indeed, it could be made to appear that a cause could be separated at pleasure from its effect; say, the report of a piece of ordnance from the explosion of the charge, it would be something to the point. It would be showing, at any rate, that, in as far as duration was concerned, a separation between the parts of a succession, might actually take place,—to which the argument in hand has no reference. This would be a most convenient discovery; as, upon the most distant intimation of any impending calamity, we might possibly divide the effect so far in the order of time from the cause, as to keep ourselves clear of the consequences. A ball fired at a man might, in all likelihood, be arrested in its progress without the assistance of Father Murphy, who was an adept in these matters; or, even after being shot through the head, he might be prevented from suffering any mischief till it was found convenient to allow the parts of the succession of events thus separated, to close. This brings to our remembrance the curious fact of Dean Swift having put off a lunar eclipse for twenty-four hours or better, because he was too unwell at the time to describe it to some of his country friends; or the poet's description of the lion—

"Who look'd so horrible and woudrous grim,
That his own shadow durst not follow him."

Of the same nonsensical character is the idea of motion among the parts of a succession. If the motion relates to duration or the order of time, a son may exist antecedent to his father; a plant previous to the seed from which it sprung; and all the agents employed in the production either of nature or art, after these same productions, or thousands of years before them. Cæsar and Napoleon, with their respective eras, may be made to change places, or perhaps made not yet to have been brought into existence.—But—something too much of this. If the argument have reference to the division and motion of things in *space,* it is too blundering for serious consideration; if to the divisibility and moveability of things and events as relative to duration, it is too absurd.

CHAP. IX.

Fallaciousness of the third part of Mr Gillespie's "*Argument.*"

THERE is very little to be met with, so curious in its reasoning, as this part of the "Argument." We have seen that the first pretends to prove the existence of a being of infinite extension, and the second that of a being of infinite duration. In the present instance, these hypothetical beings are attempted to be made out, not different, but identical.

In one sense, it is true, we should have little objection to the doctrine here inculcated. Matter, for example, is certainly eternal; and on the ground of there being no vacuum in any part of space, it must be regarded as infinite in extension; and hence we have a being whose extent and duration both reach to infinity. But matter would not therefore be the substratum either of the one or the other: that is to say, it is not necessary—not *absolutely* necessary—that even extension, or space, should have any substratum or support to its existence whatever ; and in respect of duration, I cannot comprehend what a substratum of it means. This employment of language in an acceptation beyond the reach of our comprehension, is an adequate reason, according to the authority of common sense, and of Mr Gillespie too, for the rejection of the reasoning depending upon it. Whatever may be signified by the word, however, it must be something different from matter, since duration does not depend on matter for its existence.

But the author's " Being of infinity of expansion and infinity of duration" does not suit this plain and rational view of the subject. Taking the substratum of extension to be nothing more than the thing or substance extended, (without regard to mathematical necessity in the matter,) we can only see room for one, while Mr Gillespie introduces two, and then amalgamates them into unity.

" Either infinity of expansion subsists by itself," says he, " and then it is a being : and infinity of duration subsists by itself, and then it is a being ; or, infinity of expansion subsists not without a substratum or being ; and infinity of duration subsists not without a substratum or being.

" First, Every part of infinity of expansion is in every part of infinity of duration ; that is, every part of the being of infinity of expansion, is in every part of the being of infinity of duration ; part in all the cases, in the sense of partial consideration only.—To wit, the whole of the being of infinity of expansion, is in the whole of the being of infinity of duration : whole, but as a figure. And this being, most manifestly, impossible, if the being of infinity of expansion and the being of infinity of duration be different : it necessarily follows that they are identical.

" Then, secondly, infinity of expansion subsists not without a substratum or being ; and infinity of duration subsists not without a substratum or being. And as every part of infinity of expansion is in every part of infinity of duration ; therefore every part of the substratum of infinity of expansion is in every part of the substratum of the infinity of duration, &c.

That is, the whole of the substratum of infinity of expansion, is in the whole of the substratum of infinity of duration. And this being most manifestly impossible, if the substratum or being of infinity of expansion, and the substratum or being of infinity of duration, be different; it follows necessarily that they are identical; to wit, the substratum or being of infinity of expansion, is also the substratum or being of infinity of duration," &c. &c.

The sum and substance of all this technical argumentation, is, that a plurality of substances possessing any kind of infinity, cannot coexist; but expansion and duration having each a substratum, they may be reduced to one, which can be made to serve for both. Now, supposing Mr Gillespie to have proved the existence of his substrata, it does not appear that the principle upon which he builds his conclusion is correct. For if we cannot conceive any limit either to duration or space, they must equally be infinite. But there is nothing absurd in holding these two infinities to exist together; and why? Because they are of totally different kinds. They are as different as time and place, which people, in their most common intercourse, regard as entirely distinct. Indeed, these infinities are nothing else than time and place extended beyond all bounds. The latter is complete; is always open to our survey; and in as far as the mind can grasp it, it remains at all times within our review. But the former is essentially evanescent, for even while yet speaking of time, it has already fled,—a new portion come into existence and again gone out. Duration never can be complete; we never can recal the past, and the future, as such, is eternally the future.

If therefore the infinity of duration and that of expansion be so dissimilar in their nature as not to clash or be in the slightest degree incompatible—why should not their substrata be equally different and equally independent of each other? Any argument that should prove the infinities specified to be distinct in their character, ought to prove their substances no less distinct: and that which should make out the identity of substance in such cases, ought in like manner to make out the complete identity of the abstractions to which they belong. It will hardly do to tell us, that every part of the substratum of infinite expansion is in every part of the substratum of infinite duration, because this is not exactly the fact. Although (to shorten and familiarise the phraseology, which, without seeking any advantage from it, we have occasionally done,) space has existed in every point of time already past, it does not now exist in bygone duration, but only in what is present, and never can be supposed to overtake the future.

This doctrine, however, would not quadrate with Mr Gillespie's theory. It involves, according to his own deductions, the existence of at least *two* infinite and independent beings, which is by half too many for his purpose. Hence, the inconvenience—the obtrusive redundancy was to be got rid of on any terms and at all hazards; and hence has evidently been adopted, the awkward scheme of amalgamating the substrata of space and duration, and making only one of them, for which there seems to be as little necessity as there is for the existence of the substrata themselves.

Besides,—what are we to make of another coexistence of substances, which does not appear to have suggested itself to the author's mind? To his own thinking, he has made out but one substance or being of infinite expansion and duration, but how is he to dispose of the actual existence of matter? The want of mathematical necessity for its existence is not sufficient to strike it out of the category of present existences. To render the argument of any avail, the ideal system of the bishop of Cloyne ought to have been incorporated with it; for even with Mr Gillespie's *one* infinite substance, the real existence of matter brings along with it what he is so much afraid of—namely, the absurdity of two beings at the same time occupying the same space. On this ground let it be remembered that it is not requisite we should demonstrate the infinite extension of the material universe. In as far as it *does* extend, it occupies space; and, the infinitely extended substance occupying, of course, the whole of space, must occupy that of the material universe as well as any other,—if any other there be.

Let us suppose for a moment, the being of a substance of infinite expansion, the intelligent agent in the production of all things—and all this is contended for in the " Argument" —what was it to do when performing the miraculous and incomprehensible feat of creating the universe out of nothing ? Was it to annihilate so much of its own substance as would be necessary to make room for matter, in order to give it verge and scope enough? If not, either matter could not be brought into being, or we must suffer ourselves to be driven to the conclusion already shown to be necessary in admitting the very palpable doctrine of the actual existence of matter.

The orthodox dogma of the immateriality of god—whatever may be the other difficulties it has to contend with—has this advantage, that it brings not two substances into a compound occupancy of space. But independent of this advantage, it does not pile stratum super stratum, Pelion upon Ossa, and then contend that after all, they are of perfect unity and simplicity : that they cannot be divided even in thought, while the greatest pains are in the act of being taken in order to bring us to consider them in a different light.

But here, perhaps, I have gone somewhat too far; for upon second thoughts it strikes me that there is not a little analogy between Mr Gillespie's system and the orthodox. In the one case we have three substances in the godhead ; in the other, two. In both, the substances are held to be one and indivisible, the same in essence, equal in power and glory. No less than the old dogma, is the new one entitled to the most implicit credit, and to rank high among the sacred mysteries. It might very effectively, indeed, be made to serve as the basis of a confession of faith, as pompous and anathemal as the creed of saint Athanasius. " If any man would be a sound theist," it might run, " he must above all things believe in the mystery of the dual-unity. Now the mystery of the dual-unity is this, that there are two beings in one being, and one being in two beings. Extension is necessarily existent, and duration is necessarily existent, yet there are not two necessary existents, but one necessary existent. Extension is infinite, and duration is infinite, yet there are not two infinites, but one infinite. Infinity of extension has a support or substratum, or is itself a sub-stance; and infinity of duration has a support or substratum, or is itself a substance; yet there are not two substrata or substances, but one substratum or substance. The substratum of infinity of expansion is of unity and simplicity, and the substratum of infinity of duration is of unity and simplicity; yet there are not two unities and simplicities, but one unity and simplicity. The substratum of infinity of expansion is but one, and the substratum of infinity of duration is but one, yet there are not two ones, but one one."

This would sound well, and give a gorgeous finish to the first Book of Mr Gillespie's work; and if it had an appropriate sprinkling of vivid denunciation against unbelievers, it would be all the more characteristic for the addition, and perhaps the more authoritative too; for as it stands, the system is destitute of rational support of any kind; and I dare say it will be confessed that for a theologian to have any backing at all, is better than to have none.

CHAP. X.

Mr Gillespie's Second Book—A Departure from his own " Argument."

MR GILLESPIE professes to establish a proof of the being and attributes of God *a priori*. It is only through the first grand division of his work, however, that he is able to keep it up : in the second Book, as it is called, he deviates entirely from that line of argument. But this is the fault more of subject than of the author. The points contended for, are, " the one simple being of infinity of expansion and duration is necessarily intelligent and all-knowing ;" that it is " necessarily all-powerful," and " necessarily free." Now, it will not be any way difficult to show, that these attributes are not, and cannot be, proved in the manner announced in the title-page of this author's performance.

First, The principles laid down in his reasonings for the necessary intelligence, power, and freedom of deity, are founded in experience ; and next—as by consequence it must follow—these principles cannot be brought within the range of the general argument.

" There *is* intelligence." This is the way in which our theologian goes to work,—this the foundation-stone upon which it is attempted to erect the new fabric of necessary and infinite intelligence. The same procedure is observed with regard to freedom of agency and almighty power,—with this difference, that the principle is not expressed but assumed. But while no one denies the existence of power, or intelligence, or agency—(whether free or not need not here be disputed)—we may ask by what means we become acquainted with their existence ?. Is it by abstract principles?—by the mathematical and absolute relation of things ?—No, but by consciousness and observation.

The best mode of making these matters plain and palpable to those unaccustomed to metaphysical discussions, is to illustrate them by a specific case in point. Suppose, then, that two vessels were presented to the most shrewd yet unknowing inhabitant of Loo-choo, for example one charged with oxygen gas, and the other with carbonic acid gas,—how is he to tell the difference between them, or whether the vessels are not full of mere atmospheric air? Would he be able to demonstrate their various characters without any trial or experiment; showing that the latter naturally extinguishes combustion, and that the former, in certain cases, creates it? Were he even to make the attempt, by what sort of reasoning, I should be glad to know, would he proceed to prove the facts? By what logic endeavour to establish their relation to other facts, and the constitution and nature of things? Or suppose that Mr Gillespie himself were shown a newly-discovered sort of animal, would he be able to describe—nay, demonstrate—its intelligence, power, and kind of agency,—its character, habits, and everything else respecting it,—independent of his previous knowledge of natural history and comparative anatomy—independent of all analogy and experience?—Would he make the slightest pretence to do this by purely abstract deduction, and by that alone? If so, he must be far exalted above all earthly wisdom, or fallen below any desire for its acquirement. If not, by what show of respect for his own ideas of sound argument, can he pretend to demonstrate that any thing, especially what he never saw, is necessarily all-powerful, necessarily intelligent, and necessarily free?

Necessarily free!—Why, who ever heard of such a thing as necessary freedom? Does not the paradox convey a sufficiency of contradiction to confute itself? "If," in the words of d'Holbach, " to be under necessity is to be free, what is it to be coerced? And—of what sort of freedom is that which results from necessity?" To maintain the absolute necessity of power and intelligence is not much better. Neither of these is just so paradoxical as the necessity of freedom; but both are equally opposed to mathematical necessity, and as much so as that more curiously sounding doctrine. In short, the principle of the particular arguments introduced in support of the first part of his second book, is announced by Mr Gillespie himself simply as a *fact;* and we have seen, I presume, from the reasoning of the reviewers given in the preface to this refutation, that no matter of fact can be proved by the argument a priori.

But if the author thought intelligence, and power, and freedom of agency, necessary, in his own sense of the word, why did he not include them in the class of his necessary existences? Wherefore should he not have contended that they are substances? that they are infinite? of unity and simplicity, and so forth? If the doctrines he would teach be consistent with his own method of reasoning, why did he not propound them in regular demonstrative form, accompanying each proposition with arguments similar to those he adduces in demonstration of the existence of extension and duration? What could have prevented him from repeating the same exact process in every individual case? He is lavish enough of his demonstrations, and repetitions too, where they were by no means so urgently called for as in these instances. How, then, should he have been so niggard of them now?—now when the attributes so essential to the character of divinity are in question; and when he could so easily establish them upon grounds that cannot be shaken? These attributes certainly offer a much wider opening for the introduction of substrata than the objects chosen for this new-fangled scheme of giving body to that which stands in need of none. The reason, I am afraid, is, that he was perfectly aware of the unsoundness of his theory, and dared not venture upon the hopeless labour of making it out in the form which he evidently loves best; for we cannot think so meanly of Mr Gillespie's abilities as to suppose him blind to the advantage of a purely abstract deduction when it would have stood in so much stead, and have been most of all available.

After all, however, it is perhaps more than questionable

if theology can be rationally advantaged by any theory whatever. It is such a plexus of absurdities, that, once entangled in its meshes, we cannot get clearly out. Supposing, for instance, the necessary existence of intelligence, and power, and so forth, what does it make for the existence of a supreme intelligence?—Nothing; absolutely nothing. For in that case they must exist either by physical necessity or that which is strictly abstract. If the former—facts being the ground-work of our reasoning—we must conclude, that not only matter, but every particular thing, and every phenomenon we observe, as well as those indicated, exist and result by the same necessity: that the universe and all the operations of nature are necessary—and then, where would there be any occasion for a deity at all? If, on the other hand, the qualities specified are supposed to exist by mathematical necessity, it would be impossible to conceive of their nonexistence, or even their absence from any part of space: and to affirm such absence, would be as flat a contradiction as to deny a subject to be predicable of itself. But further, the supposition would bring a conclusion along with it equally fatal to the great question at issue. Because the necessary existence of power, intelligence, and freedom of agency, implies their existence in all places alike. To imagine otherwise would be the same as to imagine space unequally distributed;—a greater quantity of space in one cubic foot of extension than in another—than which nothing can be more absurd. But intelligence existing in all places alike, precludes the possibility of that, or power, or anything else which exists by metaphysical necessity, existing in degrees—either inferior or superior.

Should it be argued—as it probably may, for there is nothing too extraordinary for theorists, especially of the theistical school, to argue,—that the moral attributes more immediately under notice *do* exist in this way, but that being infinitely superior to human power, intelligence, and so on, cannot be regarded as of the same order; that, in fact, the latter depend upon the former, which could exist without them,—I would reply, that the hypothesis rests upon nothing but assertion; assertion, too, as irrational as it would be to maintain that boundless space, being infinitely superior to limited space, must be *sui generis,* and quite capable of retaining its attribute of infinity, although any portion of space were struck out of existence.

There may be a want of similarity in the things here made the basis of the parallel. That fault, however, does not militate against the validity of the conclusion. Abstractions and realities, it is true, cannot well be compared or made subjects of the same process of reasoning; but men have often to encounter the foe with his own weapon. At all events, who is it that sets at nought this irrefragable truth? and who has most to fear its being adopted, is the test of his reasoning?—the theist or the antitheist?—Reply were superfluous. If, upon the application of this powerful talisman to the half careless, and perhaps wholly gratuitous rejoinder just given to a supposed objection, fall to the ground, the cumbrous but ill-constructed fabric of the argument a priori comes lumbering down along with it.

CHAP. XI.

Fallacy of the " Argument" in favour of a supreme intelligence.

IN introducing into his " Argument" anything as proof for divine intelligence, power, &c. Mr Gillespie has certainly assumed most unwarrantable prerogatives. Dr Clarke, with much more consistency and candour, gives up the a priori mode of deduction the moment that the wisdom, and justice, and goodness of deity became the subjects of evidence. Prove them abstractly he saw that he could not; and although, in form, he does not exclude these attributes from his " Demonstration," he excludes them in fact, by his avowed adoption of experimental reasoning. Was this example unworthy of being followed? or were the talents and reputation of the reverend doctor not sufficiently respectable to require the assignment of some reason for adhering to a different line of conduct? It is surely more honourable to yield a position which it is impossible to retain, than battle for it in the certain prospect of defeat. But his successor is a brave and determined adversary. He seizes upon every point, whether tenable or not, and if he cannot make his stand good, he at least offers as much resistance as possible to any one who would dislodge him out of it. Be this as it may, no advantage shall be taken of his illogical course, in order to blink the present part of the argument. From the correspondence giving rise to this discussion, it appears that Mr Gillespie is particularly anxious that the evidence in support of a supreme intelligence should not be lost sight of. His wishes are, of course, to be respected; but what has been stated in the chapter immediately preceding must show him, I presume, that this is a concession which he had no right to demand.

His argument is as follows:—" Intelligence either began to be, or it never began to be. That it never began to be is evident in this, that if it began to be, it must have had a cause; for whatever begins to be must have a cause. And the cause of intelligence must be of intelligence; for what is not of intelligence cannot make intelligence begin to be. Now, intelligence being before intelligence begins to be, is a contradiction. And this absurdity following from the supposition that intelligence began to be, it is proved that intelligence never began to be."

The pith of this argument lies in the proposition, that, the cause of intelligence must be of intelligence. Now, I intend to show, that the principle here laid down is not to be depended upon, in which case the argument proves nothing; and also, that, admitting the soundness of the principle, it would lead to the introduction of an infinite series of intelligences, which would be to prove too much.

First, then, I would ask what intelligence is? Is it a

being—a substance—a thing that exists by itself? Or is it not, on the contrary, a characteristic property of a certain order of beings, dependent upon the exercise of their external senses, and, by consequence, their organization? We cannot even conceive how it should exist, independent of these circumstances. "To have intelligence, it is necessary to have ideas; to have ideas, it is necessary to have senses: and to have senses, it is necessary to be material." Intelligence, therefore, speaking generally, is nothing more than an accidental property of matter. It may be physically necessary to the beings wherein it is found to exist,—yet, like organization, feeling and life in the same bodies—nay, like form, colour, &c. in vegetable substances, and even in many of those of the mineral world,—its production cannot be excluded from the class of effects resulting from material agency. This is strictly consistent with all facts—all observation; and no doctrine of an opposite description has ever been made consistent with either.

But is it a law in physics that no new property can arise among substances in combination? that nothing can result from any combination, except what had previously existed in these substances?

If this were the case, chemical science would be at an end; or rather, it never could have had a beginning; for its chief object and greatest glory is to discover new properties and powers in matter, and render these subservient to useful purposes. Let us, however, to use Lord Bacon's expressive language, "put the question to Nature." Is combustion, for instance, never produced in any case, but by substances previously in a state of combustion? The very common, but interesting phenomenon of fire issuing from the collision of cold bodies, say flint and steel, is a sufficient reply. Another is, that oxygen and hydrogen, on being subjected to the agency of a sufficiently powerful heat, explode and resolve into water—a substance so hostile in its nature to the element from which in this case it sprung, that it is often employed to put down its fearful ravages. A multitude of examples of a similar description might be adduced; such as the ignition óf iodine upon its contact with water; the exhibition of phosphoric light by agitating the brine of the ocean; the production of colour by means of mixing liquids possessing none themselves; as well as the phenomenon of solidity resulting from a compound of substances in the fluid state,—but to enlarge would only be to occupy time in detailing what is too well known to require rehearsal.

"Intelligence, it may be said, is not a spark of fire; neither is it colour nor solidity." True; but if the doctrine that would deduce the character of a cause from that of an effect be found incorrect in other instances, wherefore should it be correct in this? Moreover, to evince intelligence in an agent producing any thing, it is not at all requisite that the same quality should be transferred to the thing produced. A steam-engine—a ship—a house—a watch—all destitute of intelligence, yet clearly show intelligence to have been engaged in their construction. If this property, then, exists in the cause, and not in the effect, why may it not exist in the effect without being in the cause?

Throughout the whole range of our observation, indeed, there is not such a thing to be found as intelligence really producing intelligence. It discovers properties and powers in the various species of matter; it adapts these to its own purposes, and contrives new modes of applying them to those ends. In short, intelligence is not procreative: it does not generate anything of its own kind: its operations are entirely confined to the improvement of things and circumstances as found to exist, which may have a tendency to exhaust, but certainly not to reproduce it.

Even in the generation of the human animal, what do we discover? Not the operation of intelligence adopting a specific procedure in order to compass an end, but what I have heard physiologists denominate a process of animal chemistry. Intelligence is not, and cannot, be present in the first stage of this process. Organization must, at least, be completed; and hence the quality in question is evidently the result of mere physical agency. If intelligence be thus produced in one instance, nay, in many instances, as far as observation goes,—why not in all?

"But, original intelligence,"—I think I hear it vehemently demanded, —"how came intelligence originally? — By physical agency too?"—In these questions, and such like, now grown very commonplace, much is usually taken for granted, and not a little that it would be difficult to reconcile with philosophy. It is first assumed, that at some time or other, a pair of human beings, the progenitors of the order, were brought into existence, and had the gift of intelligence bestowed upon them; and then that all who do not agree to the truth of this theory, are obliged to satisfy the advocates of it with a solution of the occurrence assumed! In the mouth of the theist, then, what are all queries of the sort, but a begging of the whole question? What is it but to take for granted the existence of a supernatural being, capable of performing all the impossibilities ascribed to the god of the common faith? To analyze these points in their various bearings, would be to discuss the extensive and complicated doctrine of final causes, which would be prejudiced by any partial view of it that could be taken here. It will be sufficient to remark, that, supposing the existence of a god, vested with all power and all wisdom, he must either be supposed to execute his works by mechanical means—such as are employed by the artist who models the clay with his own hands—or to have impressed upon matter such properties as would tend to the effectuation of his purposes by general laws. But the former supposition, besides being gross and degrading, and nowhere capable of support from anything like rational principle, is inadmissible on the ground that it indicates an estimate of the divine attributes infinitely beneath the standard specified. The question, therefore, to be settled is, (and be it always and most especially remembered, that everything at issue between the theist and antitheist resolves itself into this question,)—whether is it more consistent with science and philosophy, to imagine matter originally existing without properties, and then—making up for this deficiency—to introduce a being whose existence is only supposed for argument's sake, for the purpose of giving away what it has never been proved he had to give, namely, the properties of matter to matter without properties;—or, to allow these properties to exist inherently in that which we cannot exclude from our perceptions, which would be nothing—which would even be inconceivable without such properties.

To ask any man which of the alternatives is the most consistent with reason, would be offering an insult to that very reason. It may be very gratifying to people who have embraced a favorite theory respecting the origin of intelligence, to ask those who—although they could—do not choose to theorize upon subjects where experience alone is an adequate guide, how they account for the phenomenon in question; but the mass of absurdity into which these theorists have fallen, is too open and palpable not to serve as a warning against the foolish and empty pride of thinking to account for everything, and particularly for a matter upon which all men are equally ignorant. It may be a humbling duty to acknowledge ignorance; but it is surely more philosophical to perform it ingenuously, than to vaunt of a species of knowledge which it is impossible for any one case to possess.

On the question of the origin of intelligence, then, the theologian stands upon much more untenable ground than his unbelieving opponent. The one, in the very last re-source, would only be disposed to admit physical causes operating of themselves, and according to the nature of the substances operating; while the other insists upon nothing else than the same causes, only encumbered with an unnecessary and good-for-nothing superintendent. But even Mr Gillespie's reasoning is totally unfit to establish his theory of eternal intelligence. For by a parity of reasoning, we may assert that matter exists; that it must either have existed always, or have been derived from something material; for that which is material must be of matter, and, consequently, that matter is necessarily eternal. The last, indeed, is by far the best argument of the two, inasmuch as causation has a closer bearing upon things or substances than upon mere properties. Take his reasoning in this case throughout, sub.stituting matter for intelligence, and we have a powerful lever operating upon the fulcrum of his own principles for overturning all that he has brought against the self-existence of the material universe, independent of what has previously been advanced upon the subject.

- But, again, if the argument were admitted to be sound that would deduce the existence of supernatural intelligence from the fact of human and perhaps other intelligences existing—say that of the dog, the elephant, &c.—a thousand sequences would rush in with the admission in " the most admired disorder," reducing natural theology to a confused heap of contradictions and unmitigated folly. The form and organization of the elephant, it might be alleged, is eternal; because these are at present found to exist, and must therefore have had a cause. But that which bears the form and organization specified must come of an agent of the same structure; for no effect can result out of a cause of a different description. Hence the great first cause of all things would require by the argument to be of all forms, all passions, all dispositions and characters, even the most contradictory and incompatible. I seek not to expose the nakedness of such a system, by distinct allusions to the baser, as well as the more exalted, of the animal functions, and all the considerations that belong to them; yet I think it at least pardonable, to state a case strictly analogous to the author's own, but operating to the detriment of the divine character, that he may either see more clearly the fallaciousness of all such reasoning as that which he has employed in endeavouring to establish a supreme intelligence, or in the last resort, admit the conclusion, together with those just hinted at.

" Moral Depravity exists. And Moral Depravity either began to be, or it never began to be.—That it never began to be is evident in this, that if it began to be, it must have had a cause; for whatever begins to be must have a cause. And the cause of Moral Depravity must be of Moral Depravity: for what is not of Moral Depravity, cannot make Moral Depravity begin to be. Now, Moral Depravity be-

K

ing before Moral Depravity began to be, is a contradiction. And this absurdity following from the supposition that Moral Depravity began to be, it is proved that Moral Depravity never began to be: to wit, is of Infinity of Duration. And as Moral Depravity is of Infinity of Duration, and it supposes a Being; And no succession of beings is of infinity of duration; It necessarily follows, that there is one Being of Infinity of Duration which is of Moral Depravity."

The objection therefore, to an ever-during intelligence, is fixed and settled upon the surest basis: but we have yet to take notice of what the author's argument would lead to, even although we were to grant the existence of superhuman intelligence, as necessary to account for the existence of that which is human. It may be stated in a very few words.

In accounting for the existence of human intelligence, if it be necessary to look to a higher intelligence as the origin of it, we must account for the existence of the latter in precisely the same manner. We may turn the table of questions upon the theist, and ask how this last has come into existence? by supernatural causes, too?—The conclusion is inevitable; and then the next? who gave intelligence to that? Something, of course, still higher in the order of intelligence, and still more remote in its agency. If we could stop even here, there might be some little satisfaction resulting from the inquiry; but that is impossible. We can stop neither here nor anywhere else. The motive that acted in taking of the first step, urges to a second, a third, and a thousandth; and all, too, with undiminished force and energy. Once begin the series, and there can be no such thing as a termination to it. It would be a substratum of infinity of duration.

Is there any sound reason, any rule in logic, to impugn the accuracy of this conclusion? Shall we be told that the intelligence to which we owe the little share of it we possess, is infinite, underived, and necessarily existing? Some proof of this were better than an assertion; for assertion it certainly is, and that, too, a gratuitous one. It is more; it is a begging of the question at issue. How know we that the

in contradiction to this principle, is,—that the essential attributes of unity and simplicity are proved by the fact, of the substance of infinite extension and duration being immoveable; and that the grand and necessary attribute of almighty power is proved from the fact of the said substance being moveable,—that is, of its acting; aye, and not merely acting in the ordinary way, but performing the greatest of all actions,—the mighty act of creation, and the scarcely less mighty act of putting all created things in motion:—This savours rather too much of a contradiction in terms to require any comment. It is somewhat wonderful, however, that in framing his argument for the substratum of duration and extension being the originator of motion, the author should not have glanced at that in favour of divine intelligence, only two or three pages back. How is it, if intelligence must come of intelligence, that motion must not come of motion? And if motion must come of motion—what becomes of the argument for the unity and simplicity of space and duration, and their substratum, and, of course, that against the self-existence of matter?

CHAP. XIII.

Retrospective and Concluding Remarks.

WHAT, now, is the utmost value we can set upon the argument a priori for the being and attributes of God? Does it possess any value whatever? If it does, it has yet to be shown, for in the hands of the great Rector of St James's, it only proves that something must have existed from all eternity; and in those of a learned and eminent logician of our northern metropolis, nothing more than the necessary existence of infinite space and duration: none of which propositions were ever disputed, or make any thing in reality for the question. This has already been suffi-

ciently evinced in the foregoing analysis of their reasonings:
yet it may not be amiss to concentrate into one view the
chief features, the shortcomings, and anomalies of this extraordinary attempt to prop up, upon rational principles,
what has nothing to do with such principles, but which must
for ever remain a mere matter of faith.

The "Something" of Dr Clarke is doubtless intended to
be understood as a thing different and distinct from matter.
But how does he go about the demonstration that it is so?
He finds something—that is, matter—in existence at present; and hence infers that something, whether matter or
any thing else, has always existed. Then, by showing that
matter may be conceived not to exist, concludes that it is not
the always existing something. But mark the fallacy of his
deduction! The existence of matter is evidently the basis
upon which his argument rests; so that by throwing matter
out of his reckoning, he cuts away the foundation from
under his own reasoning.

Allowing this undermining of his own position to pass,
however, he seems to forget that the very objection which he
makes to the necessary existence of matter, operates with at
least equal force against that of the something for whose
sake he seeks to rob the material universe of its essential
properties. It is as easy to conceive of the nonexistence of
the thing supposed, as to conceive of the nonexistence of
that of which we are ourselves made up, together with the
world we inhabit, and the countless suns and systems occupying space in all directions. The latter has, besides, this
immense advantage even at the worst, that if not mathema-
tically necessary any more than the former, it is physically
necessary, to which important attribute the other can make
no manner of claim.

To avoid these errors, and to make sure of the necessity
so much desired, Mr Gillespie lays hold of the only two
things to which it can at all be made applicable—duration
and space—and gives them substance, or a substantial support, that he may have wherewithal to designate a *being*—a
necessary being of infinity of extension and duration. But

in this case, as in the preceding, there is an odd forgetfulness of first principles. Infinite extension and infinite duration are either necessary of themselves—absolutely so, or
they are not. If necessary of themselves, then is the introduction of Mr Gillespie's substance or substratum gratuitous
and absurd; if not necessary,—the primary propositions in
the argument are false and groundless.

Both these writers thus fail, as well as Mr Jack—signally
fail—in bringing out anything tangible—any being or agent
whose existence can be brought within the grasp of our comprehension. None of them seems able to afford a single
word of explanation or description relative to the nature and
specific qualities of their assumed somethings. All have
evidently the shadow of an abstraction in their eye, instead
of a real, an efficient and absolute deity. Dr Clarke, indeed,
at once admits and declares the impossibility of our ever being able to comprehend anything about it; and Mr Gillespie
is reduced to the dire necessity of doing what is not much
better. He can only insist dogmatically upon duration and
extension being recognized as substances, and in self-satis-
fied proof, challenges any one, in the most braggart and im-
perious tone, to show why they are not to be regarded as
substances! Eheu! eheu! and this, they say, is reasoning
—this, what they are not ashamed to call by the honored
name of demonstration! Reasoning and demonstration it
may be, the best that, in the circumstances, could be af-
forded: but only think of the consummate irrationality of
any system depending upon such logic for its support.

These are the particular fallacies which characterize the
reasoners for the being of a God according to the argument
a priori. But the grand error, the master fallacy of all,
consists of the mere construction put upon a word—a word,
too, that is never out of their mouth—NECESSITY. Yield
them this, and they work miracles with it. It is their magic
rod by whose power they banish the material universe from
the class of self-existences, and foist a nonentity into its
place. They turn it into a weapon of warfare too, and their
forte lies in the dexterous use they can make of it. They

fight with it to the last; and even after it has broken in
their hands, they either beg the advantage, or desperately
contrive to make passes and guards with the fragments of
their broken reed. Deprive them of this purely abstract
necessity, and their argument becomes of none effect. All
their quaint and technical reasonings; all their sage conclusions, resolve themselves into worse than empty and unmeaning form. And, that mathematical rules do not apply to physics and morals, does not require much reflection to perceive: and if it did, relevant grounds for the exclusion of
that sort of necessity from questions of this nature, have not
been left to the present late stage of the discussion.

The last, but by no means the most insignificant error resulting from the use of a priori reasoning is, that it shuts the
theist out, as has been but recently shown, from the possibility of proving anything relative to the divine character.
Power, intelligence, wisdom, justice, goodness, truth, and so
on,—may, without the least difficulty, be conceived absent
from any part of infinite extension or duration, and consequently from all; but as nothing exists by the necessity of
this argument, whose absence from any point of time or space
may be so much as imagined, the existence of these attributes, or of any such, can never be held necessary a priori.

Seemingly aware of having thus foreclosed themselves by
their own act from all consideration of the second part of
the subject, the advocates of theism shift their ground, and
now attempt making it out by the argument drawn from experience. This is as if we were to attempt to prove, by regular process, the postulate of there being a line carried
over the British channel in the form of an arc; and then, because arches extended over water are usually called bridges,
to conclude that the one stretching between Calais and
Dover must be a good substantial bridge of granite, if not
adamant, capable of sustaining carriages of any burden, and
passengers to any amount. Or, as if any of us were to be
tried at the bar of justice, and found guilty of robbery,
murder, and every kind of crime, not because we had com-
mitted, or ever thought of committing them, but because,

according to certain dogmas, we are all " sinners in the abstract," and therefore obnoxious to the utmost penalty of human laws as well as divine. The man who should submit without complaint to so hard a fate on so slight yet subtle grounds, might, with perfect consistency, allow the force of the a priori argument eked out by that of experience, but not otherwise. Whatever dissatisfaction any one might have to express, would lie as an objection to the motley and incoherent juncture of the arguments now referred to.

But, humouring the theologian in all his quirks, and yielding him every advantage, what does he make of intelligence, power, and all that? He takes for granted the astounding fact of the material universe having been created out of nothing, and thence infers, that that which created matter, and intelligence, and motion—namely, space and duration—must possess power, and agency, and intelligence, to an illimitable extent, notwithstanding the nature of the thing rendering impossible the possession of any such qualities,—or indeed any quality, other than extension :—More shortly thus,—The necessary existence of infinite time and space prove the fact of creation; and the fact of creation proves the possession of intelligence, power, and freedom of agency, by infinite time and space. If this be not reasoning in a circle, it is a very clever approach to it. It is twisting the ends of things so as to make them meet somehow : it is an attempt to establish as truth, at the expence of nature and philosophy, that which is contradicted both by philosophy and nature, as well as by immutable truth.

Destitute of moral attributes, then, destitute of cognisable properties and even of substance, what are we to denominate the subject of abstract theological reasoning? It would be ridiculous to call it god; it would be foolish to call it matter, or give it the name of anything we know. Not more empty and fleeting is the filmy cloud that meets the eye of the mariner as it floats upon the distant horizon; and not more capable of realising the dreams respecting it, than is that deceitful appearance of land calculated to fulfil the ardent anticipations of home, comforts, friends, and enjoyments, which it suggests. The garden of the Hesperides, with its golden fruit, may as soon be expected to spring up from the vapour of the Atlantic, as that the mere abstraction brought out by the argument a priori, should be proved a deity by its sustainment of the divine character.

Meagre and unsatisfactory as this whole argument is, however, we are made to understand that the other arguments for the being and attributes of a god are much inferior to it. It is confidently held forth as the greatest, the best, and most complete of all, and the only one which is perfectly conclusive. If this be sooth,—and it is not here that the statement may be questioned—theology has miserably little to boast of. What can be said of its first principles, but that they are trite and inapplicable? what of its reasons, but that they are crank and unnatural, to say nothing of their dryness and total want of interest—devoid either of truth or comprehensibility? and what of its inferences, but that they are far-fetched and tortuous, and of course amply illogical? Theology must be sorely distressed for standing ground, if this be its strongest position—its fortress—its rock—its high tower. The ignorant, and those who make but slender pretensions to reasoning, fly to the first and most obvious thing they can find to prove the existence of *their* god. They appeal to the thunder, the earthquake, the tornado. They appeal to shipwrecks, conflagrations, and the thousand disasters that fall indiscriminately on the unfortunate, as well as all the evils that flesh is heir to, and ask if these are not the doings of an infinitely just and benevolent deity. The half reasoner; he who would be considered a votary of physical science as well as of divinity; who divides his homage between the two; or who rather—if not holding to the one and despising the other—would reconcile religion to philosophy by rendering the latter subservient to the former as the object of his greatest solicitude,—appeals to a constitution of things and an order of nature destitute of all moral regard, but where, on the contrary, innocence and guilt are completely confounded, as if by a blind and unintelligent fatality. But now comes the

mathematician to quash all these appeals as having reference
to limited power and limited intellect; as having reference to
something which (for aught that appears to the contrary) may
not have always existed—nay, which at this moment may
have dropped altogether out of being. His objections to the
reasoning of his friends are certainly cogent and strong, and
hence his mode of proof may, after all, be justly entitled to
the decision he awards in its favor. But until he can annihilate the universe by some other means than the equivocation of a word; until he can demonstrate the self-existent
substance by a process more worthy of respect than a ridiculous bravado; and until he is able to show that all the attributes he would fain ascribe to the object of his search, are as
necessarily applicable to that object as the relation between
twice two and four:—till he accomplish all this, he labors
but in vain: he only sows the wind and reaps the whirlwind.

FINIS.

Printed and Published by H. Robinson & Co. 7, Brunswick Place.

ERRATA.

Page 20, line 23, for " obscurity," read " absurdity."
Page 66, line 6 from bottom, for " he," read " be."
Page 69, line 13, for " is," read " as."
Page 74, line 22, dele " case."
Page 78, line 16, after matter, supply ?

CPSIA information can be obtained
at www.ICGtesting.com
Printed in the USA
BVHW081104040119
537046BV00016B/715/P

9 781334 008139